AUTHENTIC
Girlfriends

Also by Mary R. Snyder

God, Grace, and Girlfriends: Adventures in Faith and Friendship

AUTHENTIC Girlfriends

Real Women Finding Real Faith

Mary R. Snyder

NEW HOPE
PUBLISHERS
Gospel-Centered. Missions-Driven.

BIRMINGHAM, ALABAMA

New Hope® Publishers
PO Box 12065
Birmingham, AL 35202-2065
NewHopeDigital.com
New Hope Publishers is a division of WMU®.

Library of Congress Cataloging-in-Publication Data

Snyder, Mary, 1963-
  Authentic girlfriends : real women finding real faith / by Mary Snyder.
    pages cm
  ISBN 978-1-59669-414-9 (sc)
  1. Christian women—Religious life—Textbooks. 2. Christian women—Biblical teaching—Textbooks. 3. Female friendship—Religious aspects—Christianity—Textbooks. 4. Female friendship—Biblical teaching—Textbooks. I. Title.
  BV4527.S6367 2014
  248.8'43—dc23
                          2014013614

ISBN-10: 1-59669-414-9
ISBN-13: 978-1-59669-414-9

N144120 • 0814 • 2M1

See and use these QR codes

Special videos in this book allow you to hear and see Mary Snyder.

See and use these QR codes you'll find in each chapter throughout this content.

You will see and hear Mary R. Snyder—aboard a cruise ship, on Route 66 with her friend, and on her front porch along with pets—sharing encouragements from this study.

For more information on New Hope QR codes, please go to
NewHopeDigital.com/QR.

To find additional resources by Mary, please go to
NewHopeDigital.com

Contents

Acknowledgments

I want to thank two women who helped their girlfriend make this Bible study possible: Karen Barrows and Melinda Garman. Without their authentic, godly friendship, hard work, prayers, and amazing skills, I would have been unable to complete this study. They continue to be an answer to prayer. They are my dearest friends, strongest advocates, and greatest supporters—and they hold me accountable and help me to stick with whatever the Lord has called me to do.

Melinda Garman is a gifted writer, an incredible mom, and an amazing Mimmie. Her love for the Lord permeates her life, writing, and relationships. She is married to her best friend, Kevin, and they live in beautiful Weatherford, Texas. Along with all of these amazing attributes, she is my traveling partner and the girl willing to take a road trip or a cruise at the last minute.

Karen Barrows is one of the most passionate people I know. She shares her love for Jesus in every aspect of her life. Karen is a gifted speaker and writer. She has a heart for leading people into a deeper relationship with Jesus. She and her wonderful husband, Phillip, make their home in sunny Naples, Florida, and they have recently started work on a new ministry. Karen is mom to three great kids and grand to one beautiful little girl. She is also my traveling partner; we've sailed on more cruises than I can count and we're always looking to plan the next great trip.

I'm so very grateful for their collaboration.

Mary R. Snyder

MaryRSnyder.com
(MelindaGarman.com)
(KarenBarrows.com)

Introduction

uthentic: The terms *real*, *true*, and *accurate* help define that word. When I began to think about authentic faith and authentic relationships, I wondered why I was writing this. When it comes to living examples, I feel I miss the mark. *Writing* about authenticity —terrifying! Me—authentic? I color my hair, apply fake nails, wear lipstick to bed, and can't function without my "industrial-strength" body shapers. *Lord, I think You've picked the wrong person for this.* However, it's not about me; it's about Him working His authenticity into all of us.

And God gives grace to the humble. In the course of writing this, God has humbled me. I had to cry out to Him for help. He was faithful to provide, including the collaboration of the two dear friends I've acknowledged, who helped me form this study. Without God's sovereign influence, and their gifts, you would never have had the opportunity to interact with this study.

When New Hope had communicated a request for this study, I had deleted the email. *I* didn't want to consider it. *I* had walked away from writing. While *I* love writing, *I* couldn't manage the marketing part of writing. *I* like it too much. *I* chased after fame. And *I* fell into the pit of self-promotion. Everything became about more sales and speaking engagements: teaching, blogging, speaking, and life was getting crazy. I didn't like who *I* was becoming. God showed me that I was replacing my ministry and my relationship with Jesus with marketing. I had put book sales and number of speaking engagements ahead of time with my Lord. I had made fame and success my benchmark for my faithfulness. So I didn't respond to my publisher's email for a few days. I prayed about it. I told (key word here is *told*) God that I was done with writing.

I said this to God as if He were unaware of what a mess I am without Him as my number one. He reminded me, through His Word and through the words of a couple of amazing prayer warriors, that He brought this opportunity to me, that He alone would see this book accomplished, and that in Him, I can do the impossible—for Him, not for me.

I tell you all this so you know that I'm walking alongside you on this journey to authentic faith and authentic friendships. I still seek answers; I'm learning and relearning.

Beginning This Bible Study

Let's trust God and dive into His Word together. Looking at our faith and at our relationships with a biblical lens will help us

figure out why we are who we are. Let's set aside the pretentions, and get real with ourselves and with God. After all, He knows us and He still loves us. Even in our mess, His Word shows us that He can bless us with tools to be authentic.

Life is filled with transitions; some are easy and fun, whereas others can be painful. But each change brings a new beginning. I've had my share of changes: from the corporate world to the at-home-mom world; from a home filled with noisy teenage girls to a quiet empty nest; from part-time employee to full-time director; and from fully engaged, there-every-time-the-door-opened church member to one who misses church because of travel with work. Yes, life changes. Relationships change. But God is always constant. Within Him, we find our constant, we realize the truth; because He can only be true.

In this study, we will look at our faith and what it means to us. We will dive into our fellowship with God the Father and with Jesus Christ, the Savior of the world. We will walk through who we are in Christ and who He calls us to be. We will spend several weeks understanding friendships and learning how to set boundaries. One week is dedicated to working through tough, treacherous relationships. The last week is focused on the adventure of a life in Christ. My prayer is that we will end this time with a greater knowledge of who we are in Christ, an appreciation of how relationships can bless our lives, and an understanding of pitfalls for which we need to watch.

Once we complete our six weeks of Bible study, you will continue on with the new friends (and old ones) you've made. At the end of the six-week study, we will dive deeper with four weeks of daily devotional material that includes group gathering questions and ideas to use in getting out into the community. Through it all, my prayer is that we all develop a deeper and stronger walk with the Lord. To begin to have a passion for Him—all we have to do is ask (Matthew 7:7–11).

Enjoy this adventure and know that I am praying for you!

WEEK 1

Authentic Faith

DAY 1:

SPRAY-ON FAITH

I love being tan! I personally think I look thinner and younger when I'm darker. Although I love the idea of looking tan, I hate to sweat. I see no reason to sit in the hot sun—or roasting in a tanning bed.

So I've tried tanning creams, but they require something I lack: patience. Without patience, I look like a rust-colored tie-dyed experiment gone wrong. Enter the spray tan! I could stand in a capsule and have a machine spray on my mostly believable tan. No sweat, no tanning-bed threat, or cream applications. After a few sessions, a thought hit me.

My faith has been like the spray tan! I want deep faith in the Lord. I want to walk daily with Jesus—but *I wasn't willing to do the hard stuff to get it. I had created my own brand of faith—the spray-on kind.*

A Dash of Jesus

I went to all the conferences. *Spray a little faith on me.* I signed up for all the Bible studies. *Spurt on a bit more faith.* I was at every church service and event. I served on committees, led teams, and hosted groups. I did all the right things. *Spray. Spray. Spray.* But I never spent time with the Lord. I never opened my Bible to just read and enjoy. My faith was sprayed on by my pastors, Bible teachers, and leaders. I didn't have my own faith. I couldn't tell you why I believed what I believed, but I would list all the conferences I attended and all the sermons I had heard. Don't get me wrong, these are all good things—great things in fact—but I was missing out on the *best* thing. I was missing out on a personal relationship with Jesus.

I knew who Jesus is. I knew He died to save me from my sins. I had accepted His free gift of salvation, but I didn't spend time with

Him. I hadn't taken the time to get to know Him. I missed out on the personal relationship with my Savior and Lord, Jesus Christ.

Then a storm hit, and that spray-on faith wasn't enough. Here's the thing about the spray-on tan: if you get wet within hours of your spraying, the tan runs. When this happens, it's easy to see the tan is only on the surface. The same thing happens when faith is only surface deep. When the storm hits, that spray-on faith doesn't hold up. I learned this when a person I trusted to spray faith over me was not the person I thought. I was lost. I'd placed this person in such authority that I didn't know what to do. But God did. He took a storm in my life and used it to draw me closer to Him and into a personal relationship.

Through the storm, I learned that I need more Jesus—not more of what someone could tell me about Jesus, but more of Jesus Himself. I need to read His words and not just listen to someone repeat them for me. I need to use every sermon, every lesson, and every Bible study as tools to dig deeper into the Scriptures to discover more about my Savior firsthand. I need to spend time alone with my Savior in prayer and in His Holy Word. I need to know His voice. I learned this in the storm.

Walking on Water

The disciples experienced what can happen during a storm when Jesus comes on the scene. Please read Matthew 14:22–32. What happened when the disciples saw Jesus walking across the water (v. 26)?

They thought a ghost was coming toward them! Take a look at what happened next. In verse 27, Jesus responded to their cries. Notice what Jesus said. He knew these men would recognize His voice. They were in the midst of the storm, but they could recognize the voice of Jesus because they were personally involved with Him. They had walked with Him.

We have that same ability today. We can know His voice. We can personally walk with Him. He can calm our hearts when we are in the midst of the storms if only we allow Him to rule our lives. I love what Peter does in verse 28: "'Lord, if it's you,' Peter replied, 'tell me to come to you on the water'" (Matthew 14:28). And Jesus replied with a single word (v. 29).

This is still Jesus' word to us: Come. Just come. No pretense, no acting, no spray-on faith.

Peter jumped out of that boat and took off toward Jesus. All went well until he took note of the storm raging around him. Peter took his eyes off Jesus and he began to sink.

Jesus caught him, pulled him up, and said what (v. 31)?

Jesus is still pulling us up and accompanying us to the boat. He is the Lord of the storms, and He can hold us up while we walk through the storms. No amount of lessons, sermons, or conferences will ever give anyone the ability to save themselves. Only Jesus saves.

Anyone struggling with a spray-on faith can start living an authentic faith today by getting to know Jesus through time in His Word, through calling to Him in prayer. Making time with Jesus priority means He will be there in the storms, and we will grow.

Dear Lord,

How easy it is for me to wear a spray-on faith. It looks good from the outside, and only I know it's only surface deep. Lord, give me the courage and patience to develop deeper faith, authentic faith. Help us to be beacons of light at home, church, and in community. In Your precious name, amen.

DAY 2:

FORMULA FAITH

The basis on which I once judged my faithfulness was this formula: the number of times I attend church multiplied by the number of areas in which I serve within the church. That was silly, wasn't it?

As silly as that sounds, I lived by my formula for years. I had to do certain things to consider myself faithful. These things were not about my personal relationship with Jesus; they were more about my need to have others see me as faithful. I call it my own personal brand of legalism, and I'm still in recovery.

I think we all want to *do* stuff for God. I see this desire to *do something* running rampant across our churches. I see it in myself when I get so busy doing something that I forget for *whom* I'm doing it. I get lost in the busyness and the business of church and forget Jesus wants me first. He wants to be in relationship with me. He wants me to spend time with Him, to read His Holy Word, to pray, to meditate on Him. He wants me to focus on His will for my life before I agree to serve on another committee. I know that. I get it. I have walked as a follower of Jesus for a while and now realize that sometimes when I'm wholly focused on Him and doing His will, others don't even see it.

Whom Are You Serving?

If others can't see your faith—or their definition of your faith—they may not understand who you are. That's why formula faith is so tempting. I can serve on committees, lead Bible studies, host youth groups, join small groups, and serve in the kitchen, and people see that. I want people to *see* the work I do for the Lord—I want people to see me and think, *Wow, what a Christian!* I know how ridiculous and unspiritual this sounds, but it's the reality of my life. I struggle with a desire to be noticed and recognized for the good stuff. I want people to notice the outward manifestations of my faith. The danger comes when the outward manifestations of our faith are the *only* manifestations of our faith. When the only time we open the Bible is in a group, the only time we utter a prayer is in a group, the only time we praise God is in a group, our only community with God is inside a group, and then we are living a formula faith. It's a dangerous way to live.

Please read Luke 16:14–15. Jesus had been teaching before the Pharisees, the tax collectors, and the sinners (Luke 15:1–2). After listening to Jesus' teachings, what did the Pharisees do?

In verse 14, what words are used to describe this group of people?

How did Jesus describe the group (v. 15)?

Notice that Jesus didn't attack the Pharisees; rather, He pointed out that God knew what was in their hearts, their faith formula.

If we develop our idea of what faith "looks" like, we may include church attendance, church service, belonging to groups, listening to Christian music, and myriad things. But faith is personal and based solely on our personal relationship with God. What if our authentic faith is grounded in the Word of God? What if our faith looks very different from a friend's faith?

I encourage each of us to have a heart open to receive what the Holy Spirit has for us. We can attend church where followers come together to worship God, to be equipped by fellow followers, and to be encouraged in faith. We can prepare to go into the world and live out authentic faith.

Our Treasure

Please read the following passage from 2 Corinthians to discover the treasure within us:

For God, who said, "Let light shine out of darkness," made his light shine in our hearts to give us the light of the knowledge of God's glory displayed in the face of Christ. But we have this treasure in jars of clay to show that this all-surpassing power is from God and not from us (2 Corinthians 4:6–7).

What do we have within us?

When His Spirit shines in our hearts, this far exceeds any formula we could put together. We are simple, unworthy clay jars.

Recently, my husband and I installed a beautiful new light fixture in the foyer. It's the kind that looks a bit like a large bowl and the light is inside the bowl. My husband was up on the ladder working on the electrical connections, and I was holding the thick glass bowl. I dropped it. Thankfully, it didn't shatter. But it did crack and one small piece broke off. I grabbed the glue and repaired the cracks as best I could. When we installed it, I turned the shade so no one would notice the crack. The light glows beautifully through the shade; yet when you find that repaired spot, the light shines more brightly through the cracks.

I'm fairly certain my jar has been cracked several times, but in God's grace and love, He has repaired each crack. Look at it this way too. I've been repaired much like my shade. You don't know where the cracks were unless you know to look for the places where God's light is the brightest. God continues to restore each crack in my life. This restoration is so precious because with each touch from my Lord, I grow to know Him more.

God, in all His amazing grace, places His power within us—cracked jars that we are. We have, within us, this power—the light of Christ.

How is God's power described in 2 Corinthians 4:7?

The New International Version of the Bible uses the term *all-surpassing power*, but the terms *excellency of the power* and *extraordinary power* are used in other versions (KJV and HCSB, respectively). No matter the version, the power is beyond our human understanding. This power raised Jesus from the dead; this power saves us from eternal damnation; this power promises us eternal life—this all-surpassing, extraordinary power.

Review 2 Corinthians 4:7. From where do we receive this power?

This is one moment (among many) that I wish I were sitting right beside you. I can almost imagine the comments of, "Well, from God, of course." And I would say, "Amen!" to you. But I want to show you something I found interesting. The Scripture reads, "But we have this treasure in jars of clay to show that this all-surpassing power is from God and not from us." Notice the latter: "not from us." The Lord had to remind us that we do not do this on our own. While His power resides in us, it is not our own.

I love how God knows that we are prideful creatures who will quickly take ownership of something that belongs to God alone. He reminds us of this, to encourage. We are unworthy, ordinary jars, shattered beyond repair, but He, in all His amazing worthiness, reforms us, makes us new, and allows His power to reside in us. We don't need a formula when we embody the very power of God. No formula will ever surpass what we already have in Christ.

Dear Lord,

Show me Your ways. When I'm tempted to fit in, remind me that You are my priority. When I feel I don't know how to live my faith, remind me of Your amazing love and help me abide in that love. Jesus, You alone are the only thing I need. Amen.

DAY 3:

PERFORMANCE-BASED FAITH

*P*lease read Luke 18:9–14. Now, let's take a deeper look at this passage.

Jesus addressed this parable to whom (v. 9)?

This is the same group we studied on day 2 in Luke 16:14–15.

How is this group of people described in the second part of Luke 18:9?

They don't seem like very nice people, do they? But before I jump too high up on that high horse, let me confess. I've treated others with contempt. I've looked down on other persons. I've held myself in high regard. I'm really not all that different from the Pharisee. Have you ever considered yourself better than another person?

Please read Philippians 2:3. According to this verse, how are we to consider ourselves?

One version reads, "Consider others as more important than yourselves" (HCSB). This flies in the face of what the world teaches us. According to the world, we are supposed to focus on ourselves: Look out for number one; put ourselves first; think it's all about us.

What are some other things the world teaches us about our self-importance?

Read Philippians 2:4. What are we to look out for?

The message of this world is often in conflict with what God's Word teaches. Rather than looking out for our interests only, God's Word states we should love—that means also look out for the interests of others. (See also Matthew 5:43 and Luke 10:25.) What does this mean to you?

I look out for the interests of my family and my friends. That's easy. I love them, and I want what's best for them. But as for strangers or persons I don't like (yes, I have those persons in my life), do I look out for their interests?

The Scripture says I should look out for all of them. Everyone we connect with is a person we should esteem higher than ourselves (v. 3). We should consider their best interest in every situation. I didn't say it would be easy.

If you have a difficult co-worker, how can you look out for that person's interest?

What are other ways you can look out for the interests of others?

I refer to one person in my life as my sandpaper person; she rubs me the wrong way. Because we just don't get along, it's easy for me to be argumentative toward her. At times I have said things just to disagree with her and to upset her. This behavior was not looking out for her best interests. I could choose not to set her up for anger, but that has not been my choice in the past. I became convicted of my actions and my attitude toward her and am working on being kind and considerate to her. You would be amazed at the changes between us already.

When we think much of ourselves and consider ourselves above others, it's easy to fall into the pride of performance faith. Our faith walk becomes a stage, and we are at the center of it.

Review Luke 18:9–14, and compare the two men described in this passage.

Pharisee:

Tax collector:

The Pharisee based his faith on performance. His performance took place at the temple—this was his stage and his audience included all the other temple goers. He showed these people what he was doing for God. Often I've done the exact same thing—used my church as a stage to showcase my accomplishments for God. I've made sure to tell people what I was doing, in case the Lord didn't get the word out to them. I say this tongue in cheek. But let's think about it for a moment: How often do we announce our acts of charity to ensure we get full credit? Am I alone here?

The Stage

Performance-based faith is showing others your faith by your performance instead of living your faith. Is it wrong to share what the Lord is doing in your life? Goodness, no! I love shouting out about what God is up to in my little world. But am I telling people to get their approval? Am I telling people to showcase God's glory or my actions? Performance-based faith is all about what we do for others to see and not for the glory of the One we serve.

It's easy to slide from an authentic faith into a performance-based faith; I've seen it happen in my own life and in dear friends'. The world will tell us that we're doing it all for God, but a tiny, nagging in our spirit tells us maybe it's more for us than for God. The world will tell you to showcase the message for the greatest impact, but something in your spirit wonders if the God of the universe truly needs your help getting His message out. The world will tell you that you have to entertain the people so they have a reason to keep coming to hear the message God has given you. But your spirit is shouting out that God's amazing grace and perfect love are more than enough.

I walked with a dear friend through such a time. I was backstage at her first arena event. She was one among many speakers that day. They had all stood before crowds of thousands. She had never spoken to group of a hundred. She asked, "Why me? Why would God use me? I don't belong here. I'm nothing special." I responded: "You're prepared, right? The Lord has a message He wants you to deliver. In His grace, He wants to use you. Let Him."

Our friendship grew over time, and so did her popularity. She continued to speak to larger groups. More requests came in. She became more polished on stage. And she began to tighten her grip on what she once held so loosely. She plotted her talks for maximum effect; she planned her platform; she went from offering to God to performing "for God." She explained her behavior, saying people needed to be entertained so they would receive the message.

Then she just stopped. She looked in a mirror and realized that she thought she was doing God a favor. She knew she was wrong. Today, she's back on that big stage, but what she does there is a precious offering to God.

Now, if you're like me, you've never stood before thousands. But I confess that I've made excuses for my performance-faith behavior. I've often acted as if the world needs me to do something for God, when the opposite is true. God allows me the opportunity to serve Him. It's to His good glory that I serve.

What about you? Are you living authentic faith? Humble like the tax collector or boastful as the Pharisee?

Christ promises the abundant life to those who trust Him and chose to follow Him (John 10:10). We can rest in Him as we open our heart and *receive* His amazing grace.

> *Lord,*
>
> *Please remind me that I find my strength in You and not in the praises of man. You hung on the Cross so that I could live an abundant life. The work was Yours and the work is finished. In Your holy name, amen.*

DAY 4:

GRASPING GRACE

hat is grace? I don't want to pretend I have some great theological answer for you. Let's just dive into this topic together.

Grace is something we've heard preached from the pulpit. You've probably done a Bible study on the topic. So what is grace and what does grace have to do with our faith? These are the questions we are delving into today.

How would you describe God's grace?

I find it hard to understand the idea of something for nothing. And then I consider God's grace, and I'm overwhelmed. I don't work for it. I certainly don't deserve it. I can't do anything to repay it. Grace is mine because God has given it to me. Let's read what the Word of God teaches us about grace.

Please read the following Scriptures, and write out what each teaches:

John 1:14–17

Romans 3:22–24

Through Jesus we find God's grace. Jesus is grace personified. Jesus came so we could receive the grace of God—a life-altering grace. Grace and truth came to us through Jesus Christ.

Romans 3:22–24 is such an encouragement. I know I stand in good company because verse 23 tells me I'm no worse than any other sinner, but I'm also no better. Praise the Lord, we all stand together. The English Standard Version states verse 24 this way: All "are justified by his grace as a gift." We are justified *freely*. Nothing we do will ever earn this grace. It was done before we understood we needed it "through the redemption that came by Christ Jesus" (v. 24). Nothing is expected as payment.

Share about a time when you've freely given a gift.

The Gift of Grace

Recently I sent a friend a small funny gift. It wasn't expensive. It was just something I thought would make her laugh. I didn't expect anything in return.

I knew when the package should arrive. I waited to hear from her. Nothing. She's a busy woman, so I didn't think much of it. A few more days went by and still nothing. Crickets. We talked during that time and she didn't mention it. I began to wonder. *Did a family member get it and forget to mention it to her?* Did the delivery driver put it at her never-used side door? I asked her about it. The package had arrived, but she had gotten so busy she just forgot to say anything about it. The mystery was solved. She thanked me profusely.

I didn't expect a gift from her in return or even a thank-you card; however, I did have an expectation. I expected her to recognize that I'd given her something—albeit very small and inexpensive. My gift came with strings.

God's grace does not have any strings attached. We don't have to accept it. But it's ours if we choose to receive it.

How different God is from us. When we extend grace, we may expect something in return. God gives grace freely to us. It's so . . . otherworldly. Stunning and incomprehensible. Even so, I accept this amazing gift.

He has saved us and called us to a holy life—not because of anything we have done but because of his own purpose and grace. This grace was given us in Christ Jesus before the beginning of time, but it has now been revealed through the appearing of our Savior, Christ Jesus, who has destroyed death and has brought life and immortality to light through the gospel (2 Timothy 1:9–10).

According to 2 Timothy 1:9, why does God save sinners like us?

It amazes me that the God of the universe has a purpose for me. This breathtaking grace He gives us allows us to fulfill this holy purpose. Outside of Jesus and the grace He brings, we cannot do anything for God. We can make noise, we can pontificate, shout and spout, but we serve no holy purpose outside of Jesus and His grace.

For it is by grace you have been saved, through faith—and this is not from yourselves, it is the gift of God—not by works, so that no one can boast. For we are God's handiwork, created in Christ Jesus to do good works, which God prepared in advance for us to do (Ephesians 2:8–10).

Write out Ephesians 2:9.

The Lord knows us so well. If we could receive grace by works, we'd be bragging to the world. Grace flies in the face of our you-get-what-you-work-for society. I struggle with this one-way, nothing-to-do-with-anything-that-I-do free grace. I have to remind myself regularly that my serving God is done out of my love for Him; it's a calling by Him and not done as a way to earn His favor.

Serving in Grace

Do you ever catch yourself serving in your church, community, or organization because you want to earn God's favor?

How can you overcome this idea of working for God's favor?

For me, overcoming a desire to earn God's favor is a work in progress. If I can work to achieve grace or more grace . . . then I don't need Jesus.

Just writing that takes my breath away. Why would I ever think that? What about you? Do you truly believe your works are more valuable than Jesus' birth, life, death, and resurrection?

That's a hard question we need to ask ourselves when we think we can control grace. It's uncontrollable. We *receive* His Son and His grace as free.

Dear Lord,
Your love for us is overwhelming. Keep our hearts
focused on Your plan, our feet on the path You have for

us. Help us remember that You desire our hearts. Lord,
we thank You for loving us, saving us, and pouring out
Your grace over us. Amen.

DAY 5:

REAL FAITH

A quick search of *The Synonym Finder* gives me many options for *real*: *genuine, authentic, bona fide, true,* and so on. An authentic faith is indisputable and reliable.

We've talked about all kinds of faith this week, but what is faith? I wish I could wrap up the concept in a neat little package. When I began digging into my research books and commentaries, I found myself overwhelmed. Faith is so much and more.

Please read Hebrews 11:1. If the version you read is close to the following, fill in the blanks:

Now faith is the _____ *of things hoped for,*
the _____ *of things not seen* (Hebrews 11:1).

Appropriate terms for the first blank include *assurance* (ESV, NASB, RSV) and *substance* (KJV, NKJV).

What does the word *assurance* mean to you?

According to *Strong's Concordance*, the word translated *assurance* or *substance* means "that which has foundation; that which has actual existence." Let that soak in for a moment. Foundation—we stand on foundations; we build on foundations. Faith is my foundation. It's your foundation.

The words *conviction* (ESV, NASB, RSV) and *evidence* (KJV, NKJV) are options for the second blank. What words come to mind when you hear the word *evidence*?

When I hear the word *evidence,* I think of proof. One definition of *evidence* is a verification or authentication. Faith is the foundation, the actual existence, of things we hope for, the evidence of things not seen. Having faith doesn't mean you believe in something that is just an idea or a suggestion. Faith is founded and grounded on the actual existence and evidence of things we cannot see. We do not have a blind faith—we have a *living faith.*

In this assurance, we find hope—not the "I sure hope so" kind of hope but the hope of Romans 15:13: "May the God of hope fill you with all joy and peace as you trust in him, so that you may overflow with hope by the power of the Holy Spirit."

This kind of hope is so much more than hoping for the best or hoping for happiness or a pair of cute shoes; this is godly hope—a hope that sees beyond our circumstances and knows that God has a perfect plan for us. Even when it seems as if all is lost, this hope gets us through. This is about placing our hope in Christ alone. This is a hope that trusts God's plan for our lives even when we don't understand it.

"For we walk by faith, not by sight" (2 Corinthians 5:7 ESV). We walk in the confidence—the assurance—that what He promises will come to pass. Ours is a walk of trusting in God and looking to Him.

Active Faith

Faith produces action.

Hebrews 11:3   By faith we understand God created the universe by His Word.

Hebrews 11:4	By faith Abel offered God a more acceptable sacrifice than did Cain and God declared him righteous.
Hebrews 11:5	By faith Enoch pleased God.
Hebrews 11:7	By faith Noah built an ark and became an heir of righteousness.
Hebrews 11:8	By faith Abraham left his home and went where God told him.
Hebrews 11:11	By Abraham's faith Sarah conceived a child in her old age.
Hebrews 11:17	By faith Abraham offered Isaac as a sacrifice.
Hebrews 11:20	By faith Isaac blessed Jacob and Esau.
Hebrews 11:21	By faith Jacob blessed each of the sons of Joseph.
Hebrews 11:22	By faith Joseph gave instructions for his bones.
Hebrews 11:24–25	By faith Moses refused to be called son of Pharaoh's daughter and chose to suffer with the people of God.
Hebrews 11:29	By faith God's people crossed the Red Sea on dry ground.
Hebrews 11:30	By faith the walls of Jericho fell.
Hebrews 11:31	By faith Rahab, a prostitute, sheltered the spies, and her life was saved.

Reading directly from God's Word will bless you. Please read the whole of Hebrews 11 and understand how God's people responded in faith. Hebrews 11 ministers to my spirit when things are looking rough. I look in Hebrews 11, and I find women, everyday women, not perfect women. I find Sarah, who was too impatient to wait on God's plan. But God blessed her just as He had promised Abraham, because He is God. I find Rahab, who took a giant leap of faith and believed in a God she did not know. Rahab went from being a prostitute to being one of only five women mentioned in the lineage of Christ (Matthew 1:5).

Sister, you are God's chosen child. He has so much for you, but He requires your faith.

Look up one more verse in Hebrews 11. Regardless of the version you read, you should be able to fill in the following blank for verse 6:

And without _____ it is impossible to please God, because anyone who comes to him must believe that he exists and that he rewards those who earnestly seek him (Hebrews 11:6).

Passionate Faith

Our faith pleases God. In faith, we yield our will to His perfect will. In this faith, we will find true joy—not happiness, which is dependent on circumstances, but joy that comes only from the Lord. God rewards those who seek Him. Ask for a passion to serve God and when He gives you that passion, grab it with both hands and hang on tight. He has such an incredible plan for you.

Praise be to the God and Father of our Lord Jesus Christ! In his great mercy he has given us new birth into a living hope through the resurrection of Jesus Christ from the dead, and into an inheritance that can never perish, spoil or fade. This inheritance is kept in heaven for you (1 Peter 1:3–4).

What a week! We've looked at faith from all manner of angles —from spray-on faith, formula faith, and performance-based faith to real faith—and we've tried to grasp God's grace. We've stepped on toes—mostly mine, but maybe yours too. I've struggled through all these different brands of faith; I've lived out some and been envious of others. Truth is: all comes down to working out our faith day by day. This faith journey is a process.

Lord,

I come to You yielded. I know that without faith I cannot please You. Oh Lord, my heart so desires to please You. In Your Word, I find my strength, and in Your Word I find my hope, that inheritance promised to me through Jesus Christ. I can do all things in You, I'm forgiven, righteous, and holy. In You, I am becoming the woman You are calling me to be. Consume our lives and set our hearts on fire. In the holy and righteous name of Jesus, amen.

WEEK 2:

Real Relationships

DAY 1:

WHO IS THE REAL YOU?

*T*oday, I can tell you just who I am—a slightly frazzled, usually optimistic dreamer who loves the Lord with a passion and desires to serve Him alone. Once upon a time if you had asked, "Who are you?" I would have announced my titles—*wife, mom, daughter, friend, worker, boss, sister, chairperson, president, treasurer,* or *committee member.* All of these words tell you something about what I *do,* but they don't tell you much about who I *am.*

I have loved some of my titles through the years—like wife and mom—and others I would rather forget. I've had titles placed on me by others that I accepted as truth when they were the farthest thing from it; worn titles that now cause me to cringe and others that make me blush with shame; titles I loved at the time, but now they make me cry at the idiocy of my young self. Titles—I want only the truth of who God says I am.

Titles used to be my measurement of personal value. I rushed past individuals to manage my agenda. My heart aches because of all I missed. In all my busyness, I didn't see the persons around me, and I didn't let them see me. I had things to do—important things, church things. I was busy. And then things changed.

I found myself in a new church where I didn't know anyone, wasn't in charge of anything, didn't sit on any committees, or lead any groups. No church to-do list. No title. I was just: Mary. I didn't have a group of girlfriends to talk with before the service started or a group to go to lunch with after the service. I had my family but no girlfriends. In this new place, I slowed down enough to look around.

I loved being at church, the preaching, the people, and the small groups, but fellowship time during those Sunday morning services were painful for me. Sunday morning fellowship in the churches I attended consisted of a few minutes during the service when the congregation would warmly greet one another. In the past, I'd used this time to handle my church to-do list. I would rush around marking items off my list as I checked on this and handled that. In this new place, I didn't have any titles, no list, no agenda—and, in my mind, I had no value. So I just stood during fellowship time, not knowing what to do with myself.

And then, there *she* was with a smile on her face and papers in her hand. She brushed by me with a quick "Hi, glad you're here," but she never looked me in the eye. I watched her brush by a few others with the flash of a smile as she made her way across the room. She stopped and spoke to a couple of women before rushing off to whatever vital mission she was on. She was busy. She didn't have time to stop and talk with newcomers. She had serious things to do, church things. *Oh, Lord, is that me?* I thought. And He spoke right into my heart: *Yes, dear child.*

More Than a Title

Once I was that busy woman with a smile on her face but no time to look anyone in the eye. It wasn't that I didn't want to look; I was afraid of what I might see there. What if someone needed something? I didn't have time for that. I understood that woman because I was just like her. My heart broke for her and my heart broke for me. In all the busyness, I missed the people.

Oh Lord, don't let me be that person again. Change me.

I knew I would slip back into the role of busy woman with an all-important to-do list if I didn't make a change. I didn't want to be that person any longer. I prayed for change. I asked the Lord to give me a desire to reach people—a desire to look beyond the surface and find ways to connect with individuals. I wanted more than a group of girlfriends; I wanted to make a difference in the lives of people. I asked the Lord to teach me to look beyond the titles of people and see the heart and the needs. I asked the Lord to open my eyes to those He placed before me. I didn't want to miss a single chance for *fellowship,* the word that was taking on a new meaning in my life. I wanted people to know me, not by a title, but by my character.

Have you ever been the too-busy-to-connect woman? Circle any words that describe how you felt:

Overwhelmed	Anxious	Important	Angry
Frustrated	Used	Alone	

Have you ever been the overlooked by the too-busy-to-connect woman? Circle any words that describe how you felt:

Insignificant	Unwanted	Excluded	Sad
Hurt	Angry	Frustrated	Alone

I've been both—the too-busy-for-her-own-good woman and the overlooked feel-like-I-don't-even-exist woman. Neither worked for me. I felt as if I was only as good as the last event I'd planned or committee I'd served on. I thought marking items off my list would make me more Christlike. I frantically struggled to stay afloat in a sea of commitments I should never have made. I felt lonely and alone. When I found myself among the overlooked women in the church, no one seemed to notice me or care to get to know me. I didn't seem to matter to anyone. I didn't know how to reach out to people.

Two remarkably different types of experiences, but both led to the same feelings. In both cases, I'd placed me at the center of my fellowship and lost focus on Christ. I equated fellowship with my personal happiness and that's not what it's about. When I asked the Lord to give me a desire to reach others in fellowship, He did that and more. He gave me a desire to understand the meaning of fellowship.

Please read 1 John 1:1, and fill in the blanks: "That which was from the beginning, which we have heard, which we have seen with our eyes, which we have looked at and our hands have touched—this we proclaim concerning the _____ ____ _____ ."

What three senses does the writer reference?

Please read the following Scriptures:

In the beginning was the Word, and the Word was with God, and the Word was God (John 1:1).

The Word became flesh and made his dwelling among us. We have seen his glory, the glory of the one and only Son, who came from the Father, full of grace and truth (John 1:14).

What do these passages tell you about Jesus?

Jesus communicates the heart and mind of God to us. I know Jesus, and through Jesus, I know God. Amazing, isn't it?

Use six affirming words to describe yourself. (You don't want to use negative or hurtful words because you are God's masterpiece [Ephesians 2:10 NLT].) It's OK to use fewer words, but try for six.

These six words reveal just a little about you. Here are six words about me: *blessed, forgiven, friendly, outgoing, fun, adventurous.*

What did you learn about me? Not too much, but at least it's a start. With more words, I share more of my story.

What do your six words reveal about you? What if you shared 25 words or 100 words? The more words you share, the more someone could learn about you. The same is true for our walk with the Lord.

In six words the Lord tells us about His love for us: "For God so loved the world" (John 3:16), but there is more to the story of redemption. We have to read more to learn more. As we read on in John 3:16, we learn how God acted on His love for us — "he gave his one and only Son." Now we begin to understand a little more about God's character. We understand that His love for us is far greater than we can comprehend. Can you imagine giving your only child over to a painful death so others could live? I can't. I couldn't do it. I wouldn't do it.

We can learn even more about God in this same verse. God shows us what He is doing for us in His love: "that whoever believes in him shall not perish but have eternal life." In this last part of John 3:16, we find out that God's love for us is eternal. He wants us with Him in eternity. In His great love for us, He has created a way that we can spend eternity in His holy presence. And we learned all of this in only 25 words. The Bible contains more than 773,000 words. The more we read the Word of God, the more we learn of His character.

It's a lifelong process — this knowing God. But knowing God is more than words on a page: It's about fellowship with Christ. It's about walking in agreement with God's promises, in obedience to His teachings, and understanding His will for our lives. In Christ, we are so much more.

Romans 8:2   I am free from sin and death.

Romans 8:15   I am adopted into God's family.

Romans 8:37   I am more than a conqueror.

Romans 8:38–39 I am certain that nothing can separate me from the love of God.

Ephesians 1:4   I am chosen.

Philippians 1:6   I am confident God will complete the good work He started in me.

Ephesians 2:10   I am God's masterpiece (NLT), created for good works. (NIV: *handiwork*; KJV: *workmanship*)

1 Peter 2:9   I am a member of a royal priesthood, one of God's own people.

Let these truths be with you this week and always. I'm a lover of sticky notes and love the big, supersticky ones. I write verses on the notes and stick them all over the place. I have them on the edge of my computer monitor, on my desk, on my laptop, on mirrors, and just about anywhere I can get them to stick.

Choose one or all of the truths listed above to memorize this week. Write the verse on a sticky note, an index card, or the palm of your hand—just keep it where you'll see it. When you begin to feel like you're not quite who God says you are, look at the verse and *know* this—You are God's chosen child. Never forget that. Read His Word regarding who you are. Don't allow the titles of what you do define who you are.

> *Lord,*
>   *Let me know who I am in You. Help me remember Your Word that gives me the promises of my identity. Lord, write these verses on my heart so I won't forget them. Lord, allow me to thank You with a life spent loving You and serving You. In Your name. Amen.*

DAY 2:

REAL FELLOWSHIP

What is real fellowship? It's much more than handshaking and casseroles. Fellowship is about communicating with the person in front of us, whether it's Sunday morning at church or Thursday afternoon at the ballpark. Fellowship has everything to do with the people. True fellowship happens *when we open our hearts and listen.* Christian fellowship starts with our fellowship with our Lord Jesus Christ.

Read the following verse regarding fellowship:

We proclaim to you what we have seen and heard, so that you also may have fellowship with us. And our fellowship is with the Father and with his Son, Jesus Christ (1 John 1:3).

This is so much more than a Sunday morning hello.

Read the following Scripture and fill in the blank (referring to several Bible translations if necessary):

His divine power has granted to us all things that pertain to life and godliness, through the knowledge of him who called us to his own glory and excellence, by which he has granted to us his precious and very great promises, so that through them you may become _____ *of the divine nature, having escaped from the corruption that is in the world because of sinful desire* (2 Peter 1:3–4 ESV).

Partakers (as used in ESV, KJV, NASB, RSV and several other versions) is the word we need to fill in that blank. According to *Strong's* and *Vine's Expository Dictionary*, *partakers* and *fellowship* come from the same Greek root word (*koinōnos*), which means "have in common."

Let's glance again at the 2 Peter passage: we are "partakers of the divine nature." We are in fellowship with the divine nature. What could I, a sinner saved by grace, have in common with the divine? We find the answer in this very Scripture. Read 2 Peter 1:3–4 again.

What has His divine power given us (v. 3)?

Your Bible may state "all things" or it may read "everything."
Either way, it's all and everything we need to lead a godly life.

What two terms are used to describe the promises in verse 4?

What are synonyms for *precious* and *great?*

All We Need

God has given us everything we need in this life through His
great, magnificent promises that are precious, priceless, and
irreplaceable. Everything we need for a great life in Christ is
within us through Him. He is all we need.

Look up some of the following passages and consider the promise
from God:
- John 3:16   Philippians 4:191   Corinthians 10:13
- Romans 8:14–16   Psalm 46:1   Ephesians 1:7
- John 12:46   John 14:27   Galatians 5:1
- Matthew 11:28–29   1 Thessalonians 5:24   2 Corinthians 5:17
- 2 Corinthians 5:21   1 Peter 1:3   Colossians 3:12

Choose one (or more) Scripture promises and write the verse
on an index card. Place it where you'll see it often—mirror in
the bathroom, dash of your car, and so on. Let this verse remind
you of all the promises of God. Let's look at one more Scripture
promise today.

Please read 1 Corinthians 1:9 and fill in the blank: "God is faithful,
who has called you into _____ with his Son, Jesus
Christ our Lord."

We are in fellowship with Jesus Christ, "partakers of the divine nature" (2 Peter 1:4 ESV), and in that divine nature we find the promises of God. We find our fellowship with Christ. He is light, and we are called to be light (Ephesians 5:8). He is righteous, and in Him we are righteous (2 Corinthians 5:21). We are beloved, as He is the beloved of God (Colossians 3:12). "Common" with Christ. In our flesh, we have nothing in common with Christ, but *through His saving grace* and our acceptance of His gift of salvation, we find fellowship with Him.

Where is your fellowship with Christ on a scale of 1 to 10 (1 is you say hello on Sunday morning, and 10 is you walk in fellowship with Him moment by moment)?

1   5   10

Some days we can get caught up in all the distractions and noise of life that we can barely hear Him. He has given us "great and precious promises" (2 Peter 1:4). Let's embrace these promises and walk in fellowship with Him.

Let's ask God to increase our desire to be in fellowship with Him.

> *Lord Jesus, help me believe and understand that I have fellowship with You. Lord, help me claim the joy and blessing of this fellowship. I ask for the wisdom to walk wisely with You and the wisdom to submit my will to Yours and trust You as one I know well.*
>
> *Breathe into my life fellowship with You. Help me desire to spend time with You and in Your Word.*
>
> *In Your name, amen.*

DAY 3:

REAL FRIENDSHIPS, PART 1

*F*riends are one thing, but girlfriends, now that's something different. When I hear the word *girlfriend,* I think of real laughter and fun, of road trips and shopping trips, Bible study and retreats, and my heart soars. Girlfriends are friends who go far deeper in relationship than a superficial connection; they reach down to the heart.

In John 13:34–35, we are commanded to love one another. I love loving on my girlfriends—it's easy. I like to pick up little gifts and cards for my friends. It makes me happy to think of brightening up a girlfriend's day. Loving friends and family is easy. Most of them and most of the time.

"A new command I give you: Love one another. As I have loved you, so you must love one another. By this everyone will know that you are my disciples, if you love one another" (John 13:34–35).

Loving the Hard to Love

But some persons are plain hard to love: crabby neighbor, whining co-worker, challenging customers, the boss, or even a family member who makes you wonder how you could possibly be related. Some days I wonder why God puts so many of these hard-to-love persons in my path, and then He reminds me that I have a few hard-to-love traits of my own.

I was in a situation working alongside a hard-to-love person. I wanted to find some way to connect, but it seemed every time I reached out to her, she snapped at me. So I stopped reaching, and I started snapping at her before she could snap at me. In the midst of all of this, I was working on an article about the grace of God. I came face-to-face with my sin. I adjusted my attitude, asked for forgiveness, and made it a point to love her—not just like her, but love her. It wasn't easy. In fact, outside of Jesus I'm certain I couldn't have.

Let's praise Him for loving us right where we are; that we can love others simply because He loves us, faults and all. I didn't say it is easy, but with Him, we can do it.

But loving persons who *despise* me requires a whole different effort. God, how can I love someone who hates me?

Please read Luke 6:27–28 and fill in the blanks: "But to you who are listening I say: Love your _____ , do good to those who _____ you, bless those who _____ you, pray for those who _____ you."

Consider again the four words you used to fill in these blanks. God calls us to love beyond our own abilities. God's Word tells us we "can do all things through Christ who strengthens" us (Philippians 4:13 NKJV). "We love because he first loved us" (1 John 4:19). We love through His strength. This kind of love transcends human understanding. Loving someone who despises us is loving as Jesus does. He loved those who placed Him on the Cross, and He asked the Father to forgive them before He died on that Cross.

Do you have any enemies? If so, how did you become enemies?

How are you continuing this enemy relationship? Are you willing to forgive and ask this person to forgive you for the past?

Ask God for the wisdom and discernment to show you the next step on this path to loving your enemies.

Friend of Jesus

Are you a friend of Jesus?

Please read John 15:14 and fill in the blanks: "You are my _____ if you do what I command."

Soak in this Word from the Lord. I don't know about you, but it just makes me want to fall to my knees that He would esteem me so. Friends are precious to me and to know that my Savior, the Lord of lords, calls me friend just brings me to tears.

To ensure we don't fall along the wayside and miss all the blessings of His friendship, He tells us that to be His friend, we must do as He commands. Let's look at some of His commands. I've filled in the first one on the list today. You fill in the other commands:

John 13:34   *Love others like Jesus loves us.*

Matthew 22:37

Matthew 22:39

Luke 6:27

The preceding is an incomplete list of Jesus' commands, a sampling on how we are to treat one another. It's action, not emotion. We make a choice to love. Loving is a walk of obedience; it's one that isn't always easy, but it's always right.

> Dear Lord,
>
> Convict me when I am not loving others as You love me. I know that within myself I'm helpless to get this right. But in You, I will find strength to love my neighbors, my friends, and even my enemies because I know You've called me to love all of these. We honor and praise You, and we love You, Lord.

DAY 4:

REAL FRIENDSHIPS, PART 2

I love spending time with my girlfriends talking, laughing, and sharing. These women I trust with my dreams and my challenges. These women love me enough to hold me accountable to the life Christ has called me to live, and I do the same for them. These women are real friends.

Real friendships require us to be in a right relationship with the Lord and living a life of freedom in submission to God's will. Out of our hearts come friendships, and whatever is within our hearts impacts those friendships. If envy, competition, greed, selfishness, or jealousy has taken up residence in our hearts, then it will show up in our relationships. We, as Christians, are called to a different standard.

Please read:

Therefore, as God's chosen people, holy and dearly loved, clothe yourselves with compassion, kindness, humility, gentleness and patience. Bear with each other and forgive one another if any of you has a grievance against someone. Forgive as the Lord forgave you (Colossians 3:12–13).

In verse 12, we are told to put on five characteristics. List them:

You Are What You Wear

I want to wear these characteristics like my favorite pair of jeans, the ones that are comfortable and fit well. I don't want to wear them like the pair of red peep toes I bought that pinch and make me walk funny. Some of the characteristics listed I wear like those favorite jeans, others like the red pumps, and others fall somewhere in between.

Which of these characteristics are the most comfortable for you? Why?

Which fit like a pair of cheap high heels? Why?

Commit to pray for the attributes that you don't wear well. Ask God to help you break in those pinching high-heel attributes until they fit like your favorite jeans.

Chosen and Beloved

In Colossians 3:13, we are told to do two things. List them below:

Why are we told to do this?

Girlfriends, don't miss this in Colossians 3:12: Before being told to put on the attributes, we are referred to as "God's chosen people, holy and dearly loved." He describes us as *holy* and *dearly loved* or *beloved*, as some translations word it. Let's take a moment and work through these terms.

Write synonyms of the word *holy.*

Write synonyms of the word *beloved.*

This is you! This is who you are, sweet, blessed, dearly loved child of the King! Stand in confidence about who you are in Christ. It's in this confidence that you'll find the strength to love others —even the most unlovable ones. In this confidence you'll find the friendships you desire, friendships that will bless your heart and your life.

I can't express how much I don't want to think about the bad side of friendship. I want to live on the happy side. But, the evil one has us—godly women who love the Lord—in his crosshairs. Since he can't have us, he will do his best to make certain our lives are not a testimony to the joy of a life in Christ. The way we treat each other is a picture of our heart. What do nonbelievers see when they look at you and your relationships with your sisters in Christ? What about your relationships with other church members?

Persons who don't know the Lord aren't impressed with the number of Bible studies you've led or the amount of Scripture you can quote. They aren't impressed that you serve on six committees, sing in the choir, and teach Sunday School. Persons who don't know the Lord look at how you treat others in the good times and in the bad times; this is their gauge.

Where would you land on a gauge measuring how you love others during good times and bad?

WHOLEHEARTEDLY: You love people where they are. You try to find the good in all, but you are realistic and accept people as flawed, recognizing that you are flawed too. You work to forgive those who hurt you and move on.

HALFHEARTEDLY: You love most people where they are. You look for good in most situations. Often, you try to make people fit into your idea of righteousness. You struggle with holding grudges and forgiving people who hurt you.

HARD-HEARTEDLY: You say you love people, but you like to love them from afar. You refuse to accept anyone who doesn't fit into your idea of righteousness. You hold grudges and do not forgive others.

These are three very broad, simplistic categories, and it's possible that you fall between two of these. But what if this is the only gauge someone has for evaluating you? Strip away all the church stuff, all the community stuff, and just look at how you treat others: What do you see?

The Worst Part of Friendship

Reviewing your last two weeks, how have you treated people? How have you reacted to persons who treated you well and to those who treated you poorly? What if we could take those 14 days and play snippets of them, what would we see?

Your best:

Your worst:

It's easy to look at the best, but not so with the worst. It's hard to look closely at our failures. Trust me, I know. God took me down a road, a long, heartbreaking road, and I saw my actions for what they were—sin. I learned the hard way, but oh, how I learned! I pray daily for the Lord to give me the ability and the grace to love others right where they are.

Does this mean I agree with the actions of all my fellow Christians? No, of course I don't. I can disagree with a person and still love them. We can disagree and find a way to work through our differences with love and respect. How can we Christians reach out to those who are lost if we can't get along with one another?

Fighting among believers is nothing new; just take a look at the Galatians.

You, my brothers and sisters, were called to be free. But do not use your freedom to indulge the flesh; rather, serve one another humbly in love. For the entire law is fulfilled in keeping this one command: "Love your neighbor as yourself." If you bite and devour each other, watch out or you will be destroyed by each other (Galatians 5:13–15).

Let's break this passage down.

In verse 13, Paul, the author of Galatians, states we are called to be free. Free from what? We are called to be free from the guilt of sin, free from the penalty of sin, and free from the power of sin. We are also free from the law (See Warren Wiersbe's Bible commentary, 2007, an excellent resource on this.) Following the statement of freedom, we find a warning.

Summarize the warning from Galatians 5:13:

Next Paul tells us what we *should* do, which is in love, serve others. In this passage, we are reminded of our freedom, cautioned not to use it for our own sinful desires, and told to serve others in love. Galatians 5:14 states the command Jesus gave us in Matthew 22:39: "Love your neighbor as yourself." Verse 15 is a final warning.

Rewrite Galatians 5:15 in your own words:

In this verse, what do the words *bite* and *devour* mean to you?

Please read 1 Peter 5:8 and fill in the blank: "Be alert and of sober mind. Your enemy the devil prowls around like a _____ lion looking for someone to devour."

The enemy is a defeated foe, but he is looking to destroy anything he can—your witness, your family, your friendships, or your church. Keep on your toes and mindful.

Girlfriends, no amount of rules, guidelines, or policies will make people love one another. Policies on gossip and negative talk cannot make us love each other. This type of love is grounded in a relationship with Christ. In Him, we have the power to love one another. This love is not a burden; it's a joy. It is to God's glory that we love one another. Ask Him for the power to love persons you find hard to like and those who don't love you. It's possible.

When I find myself struggling to love someone or even like them, I ask the Lord to give me one thing to help me connect with this person—just one thing, one idea. If you can find a connection, you have the first step to building a relationship. Remember this, loving someone doesn't mean you agree with them. You *love* them—it's an action, not an emotion.

Is a lack of love ripping your fellowships apart? We must lift each other up, pray for each other, encourage each other, and rejoice with each other. This is true fellowship, and it's the basis for true friendship. As we close today, I ask that you pray for one person who is hard for you to love. Write that person's initials in the margin of this page. Commit to pray for this person daily. Ask God to give you the grace to love your hard-to-love person.

> *Dear Lord,*
>
> *Developing and maintaining real friendships can sometimes be so hard, but I know that You offer great blessings in friendships. We need Your wisdom, discernment, and heart to love all those around us—amen.*

DAY 5:

REAL CONNECTIONS

We can't close this week on the real you, real fellowship, and real friendships without talking about real connections. We live in a time when virtual connections are a blessing, but they can sometimes be a curse and a crutch. Trading a real life for a virtual life is dangerous. We feel we can control what people see in our virtual worlds—on Facebook, Twitter, blogs, and other social media—but we can't control real life. Real life happens regardless of our attempts to control it, and it's not always pretty.

Having real-life connections with other people helps us maneuver through the messes of life. I'm not saying that we must give up all online connections. Goodness, I met two of my dearest friends through blogging and Twitter. I am saying that you have to balance your online relationships with face-to-face relationships.

When the bulk of your friendships are online, you run the risk of wearing a mask. I can be whoever I want to be online. I can showcase only my best attributes. I can speak Scripture and talk in religious platitudes, and you'll never know how I engage with the world. You'll only know what I want you to know.

Maybe this isn't an issue for you. Maybe you don't spend any time online. If that's the case, wonderful! I'm thrilled for you. But don't close the book just yet—creating real connections is more than simply being in the same place at the same time. It is more than just living in the same town, attending the same church, or working together. Real connections come when you are willing to set aside your mask and let people see the real you—the authentic you.

We talked about *who* you are in day 1 of this week's study. Go back and review who you are in Christ Jesus. Now, let's see how the Lord wants us to connect to others.

Image Being Portrayed

What image are we portraying to others? Please read 2 Corinthians 3:18 to see how our image is being transformed.

And we all, who with unveiled faces contemplate the Lord's glory, are being transformed into his image with ever-increasing glory, which comes from the Lord, who is the Spirit (2 Corinthians 3:18 NIV).

So all of us who have had that veil removed can see and reflect the glory of the Lord. And the Lord—who is the Spirit—makes us more and more like him as we are changed into his glorious image (2 Corinthians 3:18 NLT).

What do we reflect, behold, or contemplate? (Note: some versions use the word *contemplate,* which means "to reflect.")

How are we being transformed?

As believers, we are a reflection or likeness of God's glory. When the world sees you—the real you, not the masks you wear—it sees God's glory in the flesh. When you wear your salvation proudly and do not hide it behind your online persona, your busyness, or something else, you are a testimony to God's amazing grace.

What do people see when they see you? Do they see your true self or the image you want them to see?

Read Matthew 5:13–16, and fill in the following blanks.

In verse 13, believers are compared to _____ _____

_____ _____ _____ .

In verse 14, believers are referred to as _____ _____

_____ _____ _____ .

In this passage, Jesus stated the reason we need to let our lights shine: "that [others] may see your good deeds and glorify your Father in heaven" (v. 16). These "good deeds" are not busyness; they are the work that the Lord has for you, for me, for all of us, according to Ephesians 2:10. When we are working in His will, we glorify Him.

The world needs to see you—holy, beloved, forgiven, and redeemed child of the One True King. In you, the authentic you, the world sees the glory of the saving grace of God. Don't hide that away in busyness. No one beyond the doors of the church is impressed with our church activities and accomplishments. Let's move beyond trying to impress one another with our masks, and let's set our sights on being all that God has created us to be.

Read the following verses, and write what God is telling you in each one. Make this personal; this is God's Word to you.

Jeremiah 29:11

Isaiah 40:29–31

Philippians 4:13

Romans 8:37–39

This is a short session, but today I want you to spend some extra time in prayer. Ask God to reveal His plan for you today. Don't try to figure out what God is going to do in your life over the next year or the next ten years. Let's focus just on today and, maybe, tomorrow. Take some time today to just sit before the Lord. Thank Him. Praise Him. Ask Him your questions. Please read His Word. Listen to what He is saying to you.

> *Father God,*
>
> *Never let us forget who You are. Remind us of who we are in You. Lord, I pray over all these women who want to grow closer to You and closer to their girlfriends. Lord, I ask that You honor this desire. Give them amazing girlfriends who love You and want more of You. In Jesus' name, amen.*

Wanted: A Few Good Girlfriends

DAY 1:

WHAT KIND OF FRIEND ARE YOU?

I love to laugh and I love an adventure. If you're taking a road trip, I want to come along. I love a good time. A good time with a group of girlfriends is at the top of my "fun stuff" list.

Beyond being a fun friend, I want to be a true friend. I want to be the friend you can call on when times are tough, the friend who doesn't allow you to accept the comfortable, the friend who points you to Jesus, the friend who challenges you to be who the Lord is calling you to be.

This describes the kind of friend I want to be, but I am not always that kind of friend. I fail—we all fail from time to time. So today we're going to look at biblical encouragements to help each of us to be the kind of friend our girlfriends need.

CONFIDANTE: Honest, caring, and steady as a rock, a confidante is the close friend who guards your secrets with her heart. Always willing to answer late-night calls and talk you through a crisis of faith, family, or friends, the confidante has earned your trust; seen you at your best and at your worst; stood by you through the wonderful and the tough times. Her heart is evident in all she does; she cares for you.

PAL: She's *easygoing*. You love spending time with, and trust her with your heart. Comfortable with her, you never struggle to fill silent times with empty babble; you simply enjoy her company. You connect, laugh at the same jokes, and have similar likes. She can drop by the house, and often does, and you don't worry because you know your friendship is bigger than a messy room.

ADVENTURER: She has fun ideas, a daring spirit, and willingly takes on a challenge. Rarely too tired, busy, or timid, she'll take a late-night pajama ice cream run or a cross-country road trip. Her open attitude encourages you to embrace life to the fullest and find a way to reach out to others.

SPIRITUAL MENTOR: With admirable, strong faith, she carefully applies a measure of prayer to every decision. She handles conflict quickly and surely using biblical principles. With words of encouragement and instruction, her daily walk with Jesus inspires you to reach for greater in your relationship with Him.

ACCOUNTABILITY PARTNER: You are on this faith path together. Some days she's a few steps ahead and encouraging you on, and other days you are leading. As friend and partner, she's agreed to link together. She doesn't replace a spouse or family, but is close to your heart and invested in your life. She pushes you to press further, reach higher, and trust God even more—and you do the same for her.

Instead of being one kind of friend, you may be a combination; a confidante to one friend and pal to another. And that can change when needed. A dear friend may go through a hard season and the relationship shifts from accountability partners to a combination of accountability and confidante. Friendships—no two are alike and that's good.

Write three friends' names. Beside each, write the type(s) you are to each other.

1.

2.

3.

Try this exercise, listing all your friends. It's a great way to see what kind of friend you are and what kind of friend you may need. An accountability friend and a spiritual mentor are two necessary friendships. If you don't have these, ask God to bring these relationships into your life.

The Comparison Pit

This is a dark side of friendship; it sometimes drives me to distraction. I don't want to be jealous of others, but I still have to catch myself about looking at someone else's house, car, ministry, job, accomplishments, and comparing myself before heading into the pit of jealousy. Have you ever found yourself doing what you know is wrong? In this area, I have to reconnect with what God's Word says. See 2 Corinthians 10:12, Galatians 6:4, Philippians 2:3, and even Romans 7:15 (NLT): "I don't really understand myself, for I want to do what is right, but I don't do it. Instead, I do what I hate."

If you compare anything in your life with that same thing in a friend's life, what is it?

Maybe you're comparing an amazing new home with a lived-in bungalow. A friend's well-mannered children with your slightly unruly bunch. When we fall into the pit of comparison, we base judgments only on what we see—what the other person has let us know about her life.

I remember in the past being so envious of a certain friend. Her husband had a high-powered professional position and they were always going to amazing events and meeting interesting people. I wanted something like that in my life. I even began to compare my husband—an amazing, loving, hardworking man—to this professional mover and shaker. In my mind, my friend had it all—a great man, marriage, home, and so on. This comparison took its toll on my marriage. I looked at my amazing husband as less than her husband. I struggled with being friends with her. I was just flat-out jealous—at least until I learned the truth.

While things looked fine to me from the outside, they were unhappy. There is much more to the story, but it's not mine to tell. I did learn a valuable lesson: Don't compare. You don't know the reality of another person's life. I learned that truth, I thank God for my husband. He adores me, is good to me, provides for our family, and is my best friend. I am greatly blessed.

When we compare our real lives with the little we know about someone else's, we're comparing real life with a person's showcase—what we see, not reality.

Investing

When we hear *investing*, our mind may turn to money. But let's consider investing in relationships.

Please read again Colossians 3:12–15 and fill in the following blanks: "Therefore, as God's chosen people, _____ and _____   _____ , clothe yourselves with compassion, kindness, humility, gentleness and patience" (Colossians 3:12).

"Holy and dearly loved"—that phrase describes us. God calls us holy. God loves us. In this love, we connect with one another; we invest in each other.

Write out the two things we are called to do in verse 13.

1.

2.

We are called to bear with one another (in other words, accept each other) and forgive each other. I love how we are reminded that God has forgiven us so we are called to that same forgiveness.

In verse 14, we are called to "put on _____

_____ ."

We are called to put on love. And what does love do? Love has the power to bind into perfect unity. Friendships are about accepting, forgiving, and loving another. Friendships are far from perfect, but they can be imperfectly wonderful. The final verse we will look at today is that last verse in this Colossians 3 passage—verse 15.

Rewrite this verse in your own words.

Peace is a wonderful thing: no strife or struggle, simply acceptance. This passage ends with the words I want to send you off with today: "be thankful." In all things, be thankful: Be thankful for your friends. Be thankful for the others walking alongside you in this study. Be thankful for all the blessings of this life. Be thankful.

> *Dear Lord,*
>
> *What a day! I love friendships, but they aren't always easy. I ask that You pour Your grace over us as we interact with our friends. Help us accept people just where they are. Lord, help us forgive anyone who hurts us. Remind us that in You, we have peace. Thank You for sending Your Son for our sins. Lord, thank You for giving me Your Word. Lord, thank You for our families,*

our friends, and all those You place in our paths—the wonderful and the difficult. We know with each relationship we have a chance to glorify You; help us do just that. Amen.

DAY 2:

SPIRITUAL FRUIT OF FRIENDSHIP, PART 1

Over the next two days, we're going to dive into the fruit of the Spirit. It can be easy to spout out *lovejoypeacepatiencekindnessgoodnessfaithfulnessgentlenessandself-control* in one breath. An "I've got this" attitude can creep in. Yet there's much richness and depth to be found in the fruit of the Spirit, when we are willing to hear and receive.

Please read Galatians 5:1 (NIV), then fill in the blanks: "It is for _____ that Christ has set us _____. Stand firm, then, and do not let yourselves be burdened again by a yoke of slavery."

Christ came to set us free. It's up to us to stand in that freedom. Are you standing firm in the freedom?

Standing firm in freedom is believing God and His Word and His intention for us to walk "holy and blameless in His sight" (Ephesians 1:3–6). Standing firm is the opposite of living in sin; it's trusting God to do a good work in our life (Ephesians 2:8–10).

Standing firm is holding on to the hope of your faith (Hebrews 11:1). God gives us fruit of the Spirit to enable us to stand firm in our freedom.

Please read Galatians 5:16–23. Write verse 17 in your own words.

Our sinful nature opposes the Spirit. When we walk in the Spirit, we are walking contrary to that nature of sin. Reread verses 19–21. This is a fairly comprehensive what-not-to-do list. Some listings are more obvious than others, but don't miss the less than obvious.

Write out all the acts listed in this passage.

Writing out this list is empowering. God is very clear about our sinful nature. I'm convicted to work on my heart because I know that I struggle with some of these sins. I know that I can find freedom only in Jesus Christ.

Now read Galatians 5:22–23 again. Write out the characteristics of the Spirit.

Underline the characteristics that come more easily to you.
Place a check mark by the characteristic that you need to work on—just one . . . OK, maybe two.

I checkmarked *gentleness* and *self-control*. I tend to be a pull-your-self-up-by-your-bootstraps girl, and I don't offer much in the way of tenderness when it comes to certain people (OK, I'm going to say it: whiners.). Gentleness doesn't come easy for me when I'm face-to-face with someone who whines about his or her life. Notice I didn't say I can't be gentle — I can. Gentleness is fruit of the Spirit, and that means God places that within my spirit.

As for self-control, I have a sharp tongue and may speak without filtering. Words in my head may come right out of my mouth. I'm a work in progress — and this is one area the Lord is working on in my heart. I'm learning to pause, pray for guidance, and then speak. It's amazing how this little difference is life-changing. I don't end up hurting someone and myself.

The Lord has given us a recipe for becoming a better friend. Let's take a closer look at each of these attributes and develop a plan to become more fruit-of-the-Spirit-filled friends.

Love

It's not by accident that love is spiritual fruit.

Please read 1 Corinthians 13:1–7. Write out verse 7.

"Love bears all things, believes all things, hopes all things, endures all things." (1 Corinthians 13:7 ESV). *Bears, believes, hopes,* and *endures* — these four words describe love in a nutshell.

Please read 1 Corinthians 13:13. Which of the three attributes listed is stated to be the greatest?

If the version you read uses the word *charity*, this is the greatest gift to give a friend; charity means *love*.

Please read John 13:34–35. How will other persons know we are Jesus' disciples?

Love sets us apart as different, as Christ followers. Not the Bible studies we lead or write. Or the number of times we attend church. Or the committees we chair. How we love and who we love. Love that bears, believes, hopes, and endures all things. That's life-altering love.

Please read Luke 6:27–31. Do you love your enemies?

I struggle with loving my enemies. But this passage directs me to do more than love; I'm to bless, even when enemies are mean to me. I don't know about you, but that's not something that comes naturally to me. Only in Christ can we find the strength to love enemies. Pray for God to release this love in you. It's amazing how He will work this out through your life.

Joy

Please read John 15:9–11. What does verse 11 say about joy?

Jesus Christ is our joy; not to be confused with happiness. Happiness is based on circumstances and comes and goes. Joy remains.

Are you living in His joy? Or are you dependent on circumstances to make you happy?

John 15:9–11 gives us the recipe for His joy: Remain in Jesus' love by obeying His commands. Stay in God's Word. Spend time in prayer.

Take time to breathe in Jesus each day before you face the world. Maybe such a time would include a short devotional with coffee, reading a Bible passage before the household awakes. However you manage it, set aside time for you and the Lord before you tackle the day. This time with the Lord is where your joy begins—and where it resides—in Christ alone.

> *Dear Lord,*
>
> *Thank You for Your Holy Word, and for lovingly showing us how to live in freedom with You. Please show Your joy to us today. Help us see and understand the love You have for us. I stand humbled before You. I'm blown away that You, the God of the universe, would want to use us to further Your kingdom. God, let each of us learn how to embrace the freedom that comes from living in the Spirit. We praise You for You are holy! Amen.*

DAY 3:

SPIRITUAL FRUIT OF FRIENDSHIP, PART 2

*L*et's jump right back into our study of the fruit of the Spirit. Read Galatians 5:22–23 again.

Peace

Please read John 16:25–33. This chunk of Scripture will bless you; dive in!

Jesus had explained to His disciples that, in a little while, they would no longer see Him, then in a little while see Him

(John 16:16–24). Since we stand on this side of the death, burial, and resurrection of Jesus, we understand what Jesus was sharing with His followers. The Scriptures tell us the disciples were baffled, but Jesus continued to encourage them. Jesus ended by explaining that He had told them these things so they might have peace in Him.

Review verse 33: "I have told you these things so that in Me you may have peace. You will have suffering in this world. Be courageous! I have conquered the world" (John 16:33 HCSB).

In verse 33, what does Jesus say we will have in this world?

Also, in verse 33 what does Jesus charge us to do?

Jesus' final statement in verse 33 shows us why peace is possible even in the face of overwhelming circumstances: "I have conquered the world" (HCSB).

The peace we have is Spirit fruit—it's a peace that comes from the knowledge that we serve the King of kings and Lord of lords. It's a God-given peace.

Patience (or Forbearance)

Please read Romans 15:5–6. Such an amazing passage this is! What if all followers of Jesus Christ would set aside our differences and glorify God? We can't compel others to do this, but we can start doing it within our own small groups, churches, and spheres of influence.

Read on in Romans 15:7 for godly instruction on how we can make this happen—how we can get to the point of glorifying God with one mind and one voice. Write out how we can do this.

Kindness

While we may be patient and accepting of our friends, the Lord also teaches us to be kind and forgiving.

Please read Ephesians 4:32. Being kind and forgiving sounds easy until we hit a snag with a friend. What happens to kindness and forgiveness in the face of betrayal, malice, and spitefulness?

I don't know about you, but I find it hard to be kind when I am hurt and become angry. I usually want to be mean to someone who is mean to me. Kindness doesn't come out of circumstance; it's not a natural response to hurt; it's a supernatural response to all things. Kindness comes from God, from God's Spirit that lives in us; it is a fruit of His Spirit working in us.

Kindness in friendships can be easy to practice when friendships are good, and it's extremely difficult when hearts are hurt.

Goodness

"God is great, God is good." I've always loved this opening line of a prayer. God *is* great and God *is* good—God embodies goodness. It's through Him we, too, can find goodness and do good works.

Please read Ephesians 2:10. For what are we created?

We have goodness given by the Spirit of God, and we have a calling to do good works.

Often I confuse good works with busy works. And sometimes I'm so overwhelmed with busy work that I don't see the good-work opportunities the Lord is placing before me. Busy work is something that benefits you as much as or more than it glorifies God. For example, you may take on a task because you enjoy the notoriety that comes with the position. Please read Matthew 6:1–4. Let's continue to do good works, quietly, so the glory goes to God. Your reward is in heaven.

Gentleness

True gentleness is from the Lord.

Please read Philippians 4:4–7 (NIV) and fill in the following blanks for verse 5: "Let your _____ be evident to all. The Lord is _____ ."

"The Lord is near." That statement makes me smile. It reminds me that God is always with me. I find my gentleness in God's strength.

What guards your heart and mind (v. 7)?

Find your gentleness in this place of peace in God. God's *peace* is guardian of our hearts and minds. When I exhale and relax into God's strength, I find peace. Try it. Pray for today; pray for tomorrow. Trust God to handle it all.

Faithfulness

Loyal and *true* are just two words that help describe faithful. Faithfulness is more than can be explained in a worldly way. It's from God. He is faithful. "If we are faithless, he remains faithful, for he cannot disown himself" (2 Timothy 2:13). This verse gives me such great comfort. Even if my faith is weak, God is faithful.

Self-control

Here we are at self-control. It's a tough one for me. I recently read an article about self-control and sanguine personalities —apparently these don't go together well. It seems the life-of-a-party personality doesn't like limits. I can relate. I struggle to control my mouth—from talking and from eating.

But self-control is a characteristic that comes from the Spirit, and that means I have it in my arsenal. It's mine if I strive to practice it by His power in me.

Read Titus 2:11–14. Christ came and died so that I could live a life in Him, and in Him I find that self-control. I don't try to do it on my own—I've tried that and I've failed. I know that without Jesus, I'm nothing. But with Jesus, I can do all things!

> *Dear Lord,*
>
> *You've given us everything we need to show others Your glory. The Holy Spirit fills us with this fruit and allows us to be more like You than any of us ever thought possible. Lord, continue to work in our lives—make us more like You each day. Let us know You more, and help us be more like You with each passing day. Jesus, You are amazing! Amen.*

DAY 4:

BEYOND CASUAL FAITH AND CASUAL FRIENDSHIPS

In the past 25 years, our society has shifted from relaxed to supercasual. We don't even have to get dressed up to go out anymore; we just wear our pajama pants in public—if we are still young enough, that is. This casual approach to life has permeated almost every part of our lives from our faith to our friendships. While I love a relaxed lifestyle, I miss some of the formality of days gone by. I remember my grandmother referred to her lady friends as Mrs. Smith or Mrs. Jones. I love the old photos of these ladies all dressed up in hats and white gloves ready for lunch with the girls or a game of Bridge.

The casual attitude has made its way into church. Now, don't get me wrong, I wear jeans to church—and that's even a bit rebellious in my church. (I'm a Deep South girl.) I'm not talking about how we dress; I'm talking about our hearts. I'm just as guilty of this casual faith as the next person, so please don't think I'm pointing fingers. Following Jesus requires more than a casual endeavor; it's a conscious commitment.

Beyond Casual Faith

Jesus stated very clearly what a person needed to do to come after Him.

Please read Luke 9:23. Write the three required actions Jesus stated in this passage:

1.

2.

3.

How can we deny ourselves?

Denying ourselves doesn't mean we have sad and unfulfilled lives. Denying selfish desires allows us to make room in our lives for what Christ has for us. How can we serve the Lord with open arms and an open heart if we are tangled in debt because we love to shop, as an obsession? These are two very broad examples, but you get the point. We have to deny ourselves first and let the Spirit do His work in our lives and direct our choices.

What does it mean to take up your cross daily?

This is a conscious commitment each day. For me, before I even get out of the bed: *Today I will serve Christ. Today I will look for the persons He brings my way, and I will reach out in love to each one — even the ones who cut me off in traffic.*

Taking up my cross daily is about what I'm choosing to do in Christ. Granted, He doesn't need me for anything. I'm blessed beyond measure to serve Him. It's in this blessing that I find the strength to pick up that cross. To love persons who hate me. To be kind. To ask forgiveness when I fall face-first into sin. To stand on the promise that I belong to God. And I stand in awe that He allows me to serve in His name.

How do you take up your cross?

What does the phrase *come after Him* mean to you?

I envision chasing Jesus as He walks among His people. I want to follow, to go where He takes me.

Where is Jesus leading you today?

Following Jesus is a conscious commitment we make. We are not perfect in following through—we are all sinners and fall *far* short of God's glory, but commitment means we get up and move forward each time we fall short.

Casual or Committed?

Commitment is a conscious work. When we make a commitment to God, we grow in our relationship with Him. When we commit to a friendship, we are doing the same—growing in our relationship.

Not every casual friendship will become a committed one, and that's OK. I have fond memories of many sweet, casual friends. We still talk from time to time as life allows. These women bless me so much, but our relationships never progressed beyond the casual.

Committed friendships are few. When I think of a committed friend, I think of someone who knows me, has invested her time in my life, and I've done likewise. I have only a handful of committed friends. Everyone needs to have at least one. We all need that friend we discussed back in week 2, days 3 and 4.

Who are the committed friends in your life?

Committed friends hold us accountable. Are you being that committed friend to your girlfriends?

If you are being that committed friend, that's wonderful! If you're not, ask God to lead you in these relationships.

I'm not going to lie to you—it's not easy. Talking to a friend about something amiss you see in her life can be hard. You might wonder, *who am I to tell her how to live?* Remember, you're not telling her how to live; you're just pointing her back to Jesus. It's not about accusing; it's about asking. When I've had friends call me out on my actions, it was done with great grace and humility. Recently, I had a sweet friend talk to me about my attitude toward a co-worker; my friend helped me to promptly check my attitude.

A committed friend may hold your feet to the fire. She challenges you to be all you can be for Christ and His kingdom. She pushes you beyond the comfortable. You need each other.

If you're living in "the casual"—faith and friendships—make the decision to move beyond, to a committed Christlike life that honors Jesus.

> *Dear Lord,*
>
> *Forgive us for casual attitudes toward You. We let life interrupt us. We allow the outside world to grab our time and our attention. Lord, teach us to love You more. Lord, grant us Your wisdom—as Your Word teaches. Help us be better followers of You and better friends to those You've entrusted to us.*
>
> *In Your name we pray. Amen.*

DAY 5:

LOOKING FOR *WILD* WOMEN

I am a work in progress. I've given a few trusted, committed friends the authority to speak correctively to me should I start acting like anything but a child of the King. I not only gave them the authority, I charged them to keep me in line. This accountability makes me a better friend.

Today I want you to make a commitment to find a trusted spiritual sister to keep you accountable. Maybe you're like me, and you need someone to keep your sharp tongue in check. As Nike says, just do it. You'll be amazed at what a blessing this will become.

Beyond needing someone to encourage me, I also want a friend who is committed to living out loud for Jesus. I want someone who will support my adventures, and I want to support hers. I need friends who will push me out beyond my comfort zone. I want to go where Jesus calls me, no matter the circumstances.

Please reread Matthew 14:22–33. (We read this Scripture in week 1, but we have more to glean from this powerful passage.) Jesus had just heard from John's disciples of John the Baptist's beheading at the hands of Herod (vv. 1–12). Jesus then went off alone, but the crowds followed Him. Jesus healed the sick and, later that day, fed the 5,000 men, plus women and children, with only five loaves of bread and two fishes (vv. 13–21). I love what Jesus did for His disciples in verse 22.

Write out Matthew 14:22.

Don't you just love that Jesus sent His men on while He dismissed the crowd? I love how Jesus cared for His people—all of them, from the disciples to the other people who had followed Him to this area. Did Jesus rush away and have His disciples handle the dismissal? No. He did it. His reasons are not spelled out in this passage, but I suggest that Jesus knew His disciples were exhausted. It had been a long day of healing and feeding. And Jesus also knew the people needed to hear from Him—not a disciple. They came to hear Jesus, not a substitute. And because of that, Jesus needed to be the one to send them on their way.

As we go through this passage of Scripture, we learn the wind kicked up and the waves became strong. The boat was "a considerable distance" (v. 24) from the shoreline. Jesus walked across the water to reach His disciples in the boat. When the disciples feared Jesus was a ghost and became afraid, Jesus calmed their fears with His words: "Take courage! It is I. Don't be afraid" (v. 27). Then Peter responded, "Lord, if it's you, tell me to come to you on the water" (v. 28).

Don't you love Peter? I do! He wants to believe this is his Jesus, but he wants to make sure.

How does Jesus respond (v. 29)?

"Come" was Jesus' simple, concise response.

I wonder what the other disciples were doing at this point. Sadly, Scripture doesn't tell us, but I would suggest that one or two other disciples might have been encouraging Peter. They might have helped him over the side and lowered him to the water. Maybe they cheered Peter on as he walked toward Jesus in this storm. Don't forget, the winds were up and the waves were knocking the boat around. The water was in no way glasslike calm. This night was stormy and the strong wind was causing waves.

I want friends who are like what I'm imagining the other disciples to have been: friends who will encourage me out of the boat, even when the waves are crashing over the bow. I need friends who will encourage me to go toward Jesus when the wind is howling. I need friends who will lower me over the side and hand me off to an adventure. Those are the friends I need. And that is the friend I want to be.

Certainly, stepping out onto the water in the middle of a storm did not seem like a smart move. But really, stepping out onto the water on the calmest day doesn't make sense either. Peter trusted Jesus. He stepped out and walked toward Him. Peter walked on water—the only person to ever do so other than Jesus. How many steps did he take? I don't know; Scripture doesn't tell us that. I would love to think Peter's friends were standing on the deck rooting him on!

Then Peter did what many of us do when we are taking a huge leap of faith: He took his eyes off Jesus and considered his circumstances (v. 30).

What happened when Peter saw the circumstances he was in?

Do you think Peter just didn't notice the wind and waves before he stepped off the boat?

As Peter sank he cried, "Lord, save me!" (v. 30).

What did Jesus do next (v. 31)?

Write what Jesus said to Peter in verse 31.

Jesus and Peter climbed in the boat. The disciples in the boat worshipped Jesus. What did these men say in verse 33?

Jesus showcased His amazing power through Peter. He showed the disciples that not only could He, Jesus, walk on water but that He also could command others to do the same.

This is the Jesus we serve. Jesus may be calling us out of the boat. Jesus may be calling our friends out of the boat. Let's be that *wild* friend who gets out of the boat when Jesus calls and encourages others to do the same.

Peter was far from perfect, but he was willing to follow Jesus. I want to be that kind of follower. I want my friends to be able to look at me and see a woman with a heart to follow Jesus. I know I'll fail and fall, but I want to be the one who gets back up and gets out of the boat again.

Will you make a commitment to be an example to your friends?

Living an authentic life means you allow others to see your failings alongside your successes. Peter sank because he took his eyes off Jesus. Maybe you've had a season of sinking. I know I have. It's time to move on. If you're resting in the boat, it's time to get out again. Trust Jesus. He's got this.

Jesus,

This recorded event involving You and Peter is amazing! Lord, we want to be eager to obey like Peter. To jump out of the boat and walk toward You when you call, even when the winds are high and the waves are crashing. Lord, remind us to keep our eyes on You when we're walking in the middle of the storm and showcase Your great grace. And Lord, when we fail, help us get up and start over in You.

In Your name we pray. Amen.

WEEK 4:

Boundaries

DAY 1:

SETTING BOUNDARIES

"I've told you these things for a purpose: that my joy might be your joy, and your joy wholly mature. This is my command: Love one another the way I loved you. This is the very best way to love. Put your life on the line for your friends. You are my friends when you do the things I command you. I'm no longer calling you servants because servants don't understand what their master is thinking and planning. No, I've named you friends because I've let you in on everything I've heard from the Father." (John 15:11–15 THE MESSAGE).

*H*onestly, we each have at least one person in our lives, possibly even a friend, who causes us pain or discomfort—someone we would rather not love, even be around. Maybe being with this person causes us to want to put up a fence with a sign that says, *No Trespassing!* My friend Karen told me:

> If I had a No Trespassing sign, I would have hung it on the front door recently—even with a good friend trying to help! While I had made plans to meet someone from my church at the local coffee shop, I frankly should never have made the appointment. My calendar was full, and it was wrong to think I could squeeze in one more meeting. The night before the planned meeting, I texted this friend to let her know I had overbooked myself and couldn't make it, asking to reschedule.
>
> The next morning, as I was sitting at my kitchen table, head down and typing furiously on the computer to meet a deadline, hair in a ponytail, and still in my pajamas, the doorbell rang. Yes, it was the friend I had texted the night before! While she was ringing the doorbell, she was also texting me to

say she was out front with coffee for two! I literally dropped to the floor and hid! Yes, hiding under the kitchen table.

We can all agree that so much is wrong in this story. First, I should never have made the appointment, and second, I should have explained that I needed a boundary. This friend had wonderful intentions, she had the right heart, but she was unclear about the boundary.

In the space below, and in your own words, please write what you think a boundary is. The goal here is not to get the right answer. The goal is for you to search your heart and write in your own words your understanding of what a boundary is.

I believe a boundary is

Next, let's look at your friendships. Who are your friends? List their first names here:

"As iron sharpens iron, so a friend sharpens a friend" (Proverbs 27:17 NLT). Iron-sharpening friendships are ones in which the friends are committed to the relationship and show their love in sacrificial ways. When healthy boundaries are in place, friends can count on each other for honest input. These friends won't say yes or agree with each other to keep each other happy. They are willing to have difficult conversations because they love and care for each other. These same friends can count on each other for encouragement and support.

Let's go a little deeper into your friendships. Review your list of friends, and consider the questions for each relationship.

Is my friendship with _____ sharpening both of us?

How am I being sharpened by my friendship with _____?

Do we have healthy boundaries? ❑ Yes ❑ No

What are the traits in our friendship that have made it successful?

Looking at your list of friends, is one particularly difficult to love, and why?

Does it seem like no matter how much you have prayed for this person, whenever you are together, one of you ends up walking away hurt or angry? Would you consider this friendship to be healthy or unhealthy?

These questions can be tough, and for some of us, this day's study can be painful. Maybe, like me, you grew up without healthy boundaries, and you've been taught that having boundaries is selfish. Maybe when you hear someone say he or she needs to set a boundary with you, your mind hears that you are unloved, or rejected, without value. God's Word gives us a biblical under-standing of boundaries, and we can move forward in loving and being loved by the friendships God has given us.

When performed with a pure heart and the right motivation, setting boundaries sends a message that we value our relationships. This is true for our family members and our friendships. Loving and healthy boundaries help to define expectations and say to the other person, "I not only love you, but I respect you." Boundaries begin with love.

At the beginning of this day's study, we opened with a passage from John 15 in which we see Jesus preparing His disciples for His departure. Earlier in that chapter, He was teaching His disciples the importance of abiding in Him. Jesus wanted His disciples then—and those of us who follow Him today—to understand that only by abiding in Him are we able to accomplish what we have been chosen by God to do: *to bear His image and to love and respect the very people He has placed in our paths.*

People are messy. Yes, that includes each of us. We are messy and flawed. Yet God has placed us in each other's lives to be His image bearers for our good and His glory.

As you look at your circle of friends, you see that you are closer to some than others. That's exactly as it should be. You can't be everyone's best friend. Friendships come in different degrees. Friendships may have to endure difficult days, but with healthy boundaries, these very same friendships will prosper and bring great fruit, not only to you and your friends but also to people outside of your circle of friends.

"Two people are better off than one, for they can help each other succeed. If one person falls, the other can reach out and help. But someone who falls alone is in real trouble" (Ecclesiastes 4:9–10 NLT).

The following are questions to consider in your friendships:

Do you and your friend pray together?

How is God glorified by your friendship?

While friends can be a huge blessing, they can also bring us pain. When you let someone into your life, you run the risk of letting that person hurt you. I'm sure we all have at least one story of being hurt or rejected by a friend from the past. Unfortunately, some of us have many stories. Because of the hurt, you may have decided you don't want a close friend. Don't close yourself off to everyone, but be careful where you place your trust. Ask God for direction. He will grant it.

The opposite of the woman who shuts herself off from the crowd is the one who is friends with everyone. She may even think she's everyone's best friend. The problem is flawed boundaries—well, flawed boundaries and out-of-balance relationships.

Perhaps you're relating to this story. If so, that's really good news and something to be celebrated. God is speaking. Thank God for His love, and confess to Him those friendships that are out of balance. As we talk with God, He will give us grace in this moment and He will lovingly lead us in our friendships.

From one man he made all the nations, that they should inhabit the whole earth; and he marked out their appointed times in history and the boundaries of their lands (Acts 17:26).

From one man he created all the nations throughout the whole earth. He decided beforehand when they should rise and fall, and he determined their boundaries (Acts 17:26 NLT).

Boundary

Boundary: Something that indicates bounds or limits; a limiting or bounding line

In Acts 17:26, the Apostle Paul explained to the men in Athens that they were descendants of Adam and that God has determined the nations and their boundaries. Paul wanted them to understand that God, in His sovereignty, rules over *all* nations and people.

God has *chosen* and *placed* us in our family and given us each friendship we have. Long before we were born, God designed us to be in relationships with one another and to live in community.

Each day this week will reveal more about your list of friends and what changes need to be made in your boundaries so that God is glorified and you begin to look more like Jesus.

This is an area we struggle with, but God can use relationships for our good, even helping us to work through messy, flawed relationships, to bring change to us and glory to Him. Let's close this day of boundary discussion with hearts full of thanks to our God. He really does love us and is looking out for our good!

> *Father God, thank You so much for Your love. Thank You for Your Son, Jesus Christ: His life, death, and resurrection. And, thank You for the friends You have placed in our lives. God, we desire to glorify You in our friendships. Please reveal what is offensive in us and show us where we need to make changes in our boundaries. In Jesus' name, amen.*

DAY 2:

OUT OF BALANCE

A couple of years ago, my friend Karen Barrows and I were on the Girls Getaway Cruise. Early one Sunday morning, we were making our way to the theater for an event. Karen had a million things running through her mind, and she wasn't giving her full attention to where we were going. All of a sudden, she tripped, lost her balance, and landed *hard* on that marble floor. Good gravy, she was horribly embarrassed and in pain. Karen recalls,

> Do you know what Mary did? She didn't laugh. She didn't leave me and rush off to the event. Instead, she threw the many things she was carrying to the side and sat right down on that marble floor next to me. She said, "Well, we will just sit in the mess together!"

We all need a friend who will just sit with us in our mess, but we also need that friend to help us out of our mess, possibly by offering a hand or a strong word. But when a friend encourages us to stay in a mess, that is an out-of-balance relationship. God doesn't call us into something that won't glorify Him.

Please read Ephesians 5:1–2:

Therefore be imitators of God, as beloved children. And walk in love, as Christ loved us and gave himself up for us, a fragrant offering and sacrifice to God (Ephesians 5:1–2 ESV).

In the Book of Ephesians, the Apostle Paul urges us to become imitators of God. What does it look like to imitate God?

Let's turn to Exodus 34:6, in which we see God revealing Himself to Moses.

To help with retention, please write out Exodus 34:6 here:

What characteristics of God were revealed through this Scripture?

The Holman Christian Standard Bible offers this translation: "Then the LORD passed in front of him and proclaimed:

Yahweh—Yahweh is a compassionate and gracious God, slow to anger and rich in faithful love and truth" (Exodus 34:6 HCSB). God uses His covenant name of Yahweh. Fill in the following blanks using this version.

Yahweh—Yahweh is a _____ and _____ God, _____ to _____ and _____ in _____ love and _____. (HCSB)

Now, remembering that we are to be imitators of God, let's apply this Scripture to our friendships. Remember that list of friends you made during yesterday's study? Would you say that your friendships are an imitation of God's love? If so, why are they?

Are you walking in love with one another, or can it be that you are no longer walking in step with one another. Has the friendship become out of balance?

As sisters in Christ our great desire is to glorify God by loving our sisters well. But, one problem is that we live in a fallen world with other messy people, and another problem is that we have an enemy who would like nothing more than to distract us, trip us, and cause us to lose our balance.

Distraction: Something that prevents someone from giving full attention to something else.

It's time to get transparent. The reason we study God's Word and attend Bible studies is so that we can be changed. Ask yourself whether you have a friend who has distracted you from God. When you asked that question, did the face of one of your friends come to mind?

It's very possible that the enemy has distracted you and, until now, you didn't even realize a friendship was out of balance. A lot of times, our minds are so preoccupied with other things that we don't even realize we've been distracted. If the Holy Spirit has convicted you of a relationship that is out of balance, pause here.

You have a God who loves you and is jealous for you. Repent of allowing this friendship to take priority over God. God will forgive you *and* will lovingly redeem you.

Please read Deuteronomy 5:33. In your own words write what Moses told the Israelites.

Once again, Scripture reveals God's compassion and love for His people. By God's grace, we are forgiven and given a new beginning, again. *Repent* means to turn away from the sin, to do things differently. This doesn't mean you have to end the friendship that has become out of balance, but it does mean that you and your friend have work to do. Changes need to be made, so that God is glorified in the relationship. Remember, we set healthy boundaries because we love and respect one another. I encourage you to sit down with your friend and share with her what God has shown you about being out of balance. Make sure to open the conversation in prayer, and ask the Holy Spirit to reveal the changes that need to be made in this relationship. As you both keep your focus on Jesus, He will give you grace in that moment.

> *Father God, You overwhelm us with Your great love for us. Thank You for giving us healthy friendships and also revealing when and where we need to make changes. Thank You so much for being a kind and compassionate God and for showing us tremendous patience. We love You so much, and we want our friendships to be a light for You in this world. In Jesus' name, amen.*

DAY 3:

Problems with Perspective

A couple of days ago when we started this chapter on boundaries, I shared with you Karen's story about a friend who showed up unannounced with coffee, ringing the doorbell. And what did she do? She hid. I wish I were kidding, but I'm not. She did not answer the door. She was under a tight deadline and knew that answering the door, it would delay the project and also have an impact on other persons depending on her. Her heart was to glorify God by finishing the project. So eventually, after about ten minutes, Karen climbed back into her chair, thanked God for that friend who cared enough to come over, and went back to work. That sweet friend had no idea Karen was under a project deadline. Her heart and desire was to bless Karen.

Welcome with open arms fellow believers who don't see things the way you do. And don't jump all over them every time they do or say something you don't agree with — even when it seems that they are strong on opinions but weak in the faith department. Remember, they have their own history to deal with. Treat them gently (Romans 14:1 The Message).

Please read Romans 14:1–12. This is a powerful passage in which we see Paul teaching us how to live free in Christ. This text also shows us that we are not to judge one another. Oftentimes, you and a friend may deal with the same situation in completely different ways. Both you and your friend may very well be within God's will. You just have different perspectives.

Read Romans 12:3–8, and complete the sentences below the passage.

For by the grace given to me, I tell everyone among you not to think of himself more highly than he should think. Instead, think sensibly, as God has distributed a measure of faith to each one. Now as we have many parts in one body, and all the parts do not have the same function, in the same way we who are many are one body in Christ and individually members of one another. According to the grace given to us, we have different gifts:

If prophecy, use it according to the standard of one's faith; if service, in service; if teaching, in teaching; if exhorting, in exhortation; giving, with generosity; leading, with diligence; showing mercy, with cheerfulness (Romans 12:3–8 HCSB)

Because of the _____ given to us, we should not think more highly of _____ .

Instead, we believe that God has given a measure of faith to _____.

We are _____ body with _____ parts. And, we do not all have the _____ function.

According to the _____ given to us, we have different _____.

It has been a great blessing to work through this day's study with you. The Lord has stirred in my heart to call that friend who was at my door a few days ago. Has He stirred anything in your heart?

Let's end this day in prayer by writing our own prayer to God. Please journal what God is saying to you, thanking Him for His grace.

DAY 4:

SURVIVING COMPETITION AND JEALOUSY, PART 1

As I think about today's topics, competition and jealousy, I thank God for the work He is doing in my heart, and I pray in your heart as well. I've been in the corporate sales world, and I've served in a Christian ministry. I've been on both sides of competition and both sides of jealousy. When you mix together women, competition, and jealousy, hearts get hurt, feelings get trampled, lives are impacted, and division occurs. It's downright ugly because competition and jealously can result in sin and sin, as we well know, is ugly.

The Book of Genesis records a story of jealousy and competition in the family of a man named Jacob. Jacob deceived his father so that he was able to steal the blessing due his brother, Esau. When Esau found out what Jacob had done, he became furious and planned to kill his brother. So Jacob fled his home to stay with his mother's brother, Laban. Laban had two daughters, Leah and Rachel. Scripture tells us that Rachel, the younger, was beautiful, but Leah was not so much so. Let's pick up the story together in Genesis 29.

Read Genesis 29:13–35. How does the story of Jacob, Leah, and Rachel make you feel?

Laban's goal for his daughters was that they both be married, the older first, so he deceived Jacob into marrying Leah. Keep in mind that Jacob had just completed seven years of working for Laban to be allowed to marry Rachel. And what did Laban do? He threw a party, and Jacob ended up marrying and having sex with Leah, the sister who was not beautiful by the world's standards. To have Rachel as his wife, Jacob would have to serve Laban another seven years.

Why do you think God allowed Laban to deceive Jacob?

Jacob didn't choose Leah. God did. You see, Leah was a picture of the way Christ would come—despised, rejected, no beauty—yet, God showed her favor. In fact, God chose her to carry on the righteous line; the Messiah would eventually come through her lineage. Long before Laban deceived Jacob, God knew Jacob would marry Leah.

As we look at Jacob's story, what do we learn about the women in Jacob's life?

Leah:

Rachel:

Here is my list for each woman:

LEAH: unattractive, rejected, unloved (Genesis 29:31), used by men (her father and her husband)

RACHEL: favored; beautiful; her fiancé was deceived into marrying her older sister (expected to be first and truly desired wife of Jacob, but became his second wife, second to her older sister); loved by Jacob (Genesis 29:30); barren, her beauty could not give her children; jealous of the older, unattractive sister who was able to have children (30:1)

In the lives of these two women, we see relationships that are marked by favortism, rejection, and jealousy: Jacob favored Rachel. Jacob rejected Leah. Leah and Rachel were jealous of each other.

In each of these relationships, we see Rachel and Leah looking to someone or something other than God to satisfy them.

Friendships can move from companionship to competition in a blink of an eye. When we begin to compare our whatever with hers, we can come up short, and then jealousy slips into the picture. Be on guard against this.

Let's look at that list of friends one more time — remember, that list we made at the beginning of this week's study. Looking at each one of those friends, determine whether you feel you are competing with any of them. Do you feel jealousy toward any of them?

If you find yourself dealing with competition, say no to the ugly. If that sounds simple and easy, it's neither. Saying no to those feelings of competition and jealousy requires diligence and trust in the Lord. Ask God for wisdom to walk through these emotions. And hold John 13:34–35 close to your heart, reminding yourself that Jesus calls us to *"love* one another."

> *God, we come to You so very thankful for the gospel: for the life, death, and resurrection of our Lord Jesus. Only the love of Christ can change our hearts and make us truly different from the inside out. Father, I pray that we gain a deeper appreciation and respect for the friends with whom You have placed us. Give us a great desire to*

love Your people well. May we respect their boundaries
and not judge them when they look different from ours.
Remind us that we are created in Your image and that
we are all different and all precious to You. Lord, we
love You and we praise You. In Jesus' name, amen.

DAY 5:

SURVIVING COMPETITION AND JEALOUSY, PART 2

Yesterday, we learned about Jacob and his wives, Leah and Rachel. We saw relationships marked by competition, jealousy, and rejection. We don't like to admit it, but we can be a lot like Leah and Rachel. We may deceive and pretend with one another. Maybe we don't lie, but we stay silent out of fear of rejection or being unloved.

By God's grace, I pray that as we have looked at our friendships during this week's study, we have started to see our own hearts and the changes we need to make in our own lives. We are all messy, and we are all sinners. Real examples of messy relationships and sinners abound in the Bible. Even the disciples competed for a place of honor in God's kingdom.

According Paul's teachings in Galatians 5, we are led either by the Holy Spirit or by our flesh. He spells out the results of each path. Please read the following passage from *The Message* to see the results of being led by the flesh:

It is obvious what kind of life develops out of trying to get your own way all the time: repetitive, loveless, cheap sex; a stinking accumulation of mental and emotional garbage; frenzied and joyless grabs for happiness; trinket gods; magic-show religion; paranoid loneliness; cutthroat competition; all-consuming-yet-never-satisfied wants; a brutal temper; an impotence to love or be loved; divided homes and divided lives; small-minded and lopsided pursuits; the vicious habit of depersonalizing everyone into a rival; uncontrolled and uncontrollable addictions; ugly parodies of community. I could go on.

This isn't the first time I have warned you, you know. If you use your freedom this way, you will not inherit God's kingdom (Galatians 5:19–21 THE MESSAGE).

Now *that* was a hard word. Those of us who have trusted Jesus Christ as our Lord and Savior need to heed Paul's warning against the acts of the sinful nature. We are not to use our freedom in Christ in these ways. God wants us to know that we are not on our own here. He is here with us and actually dwells inside us. As followers of Jesus Christ, our life is judged not by our performance, how well we know Scripture, how often we attend Bible study, how much we serve, or even how much we tithe. Our lives are evaluated by how closely we resemble our Savior.

Share how the Spirit is leading your friendships.

What has the Spirit revealed about boundaries that need to be made or changed?

Let's review Jesus' new love commandment again: "A new command I give you: Love one another. As I have loved you, so you must love one another. By this everyone will know that you are my disciples, if you love one another" (John 13:34–35).

As we end this week on boundaries, let me share again from my friend Karen:

> I'm in a very precious place with our Lord. Mary had asked me to write this during some very difficult

circumstances in my life, circumstances that often had me facedown before the Lord, crying out in pain. I'm so very thankful that I've shared this week with you in the study of God's Word. It has kept my focus on God; it has reminded me of His great love for me. I know, firsthand, that whatever you're going through, God is bigger than that. Circumstances that He causes or allows in your life really are for your good, even when you can't see it.

Over the last few weeks, I've had to open my borders, extend my boundaries, and in so doing, I've experienced the church and God's love in fresh new ways. To close our week together, will you please read the following Scripture out loud (yes, out loud).

LORD, you alone are my portion and my cup; you make my lot secure. The boundary lines have fallen for me in pleasant places; surely I have a delightful inheritance. I will praise the LORD, who counsels me; even at night my heart instructs me. I keep my eyes always on the LORD. With him at my right hand, I will not be shaken (Psalm 16:5–8).

WEEK 5:

Treacherous Ties

DAY 1:

TOXIC FRIENDSHIPS

𝓘n *The Old Testament Speaks,* Dr. Samuel Schultz notes that the psalms "express the common experience of the human race . . . the emotions, personal feelings, attitudes, gratitude, and interests of the average individual. Universally, people have identified their lot in life with that of the psalmists."

Consider Psalm 55. As you read this psalm, can you identify, feel David's pain of being betrayed by a close friend? We do not know for certain the identity of this friend, but many scholars believe it was Ahithophel, a close advisor and intimate friend to David — before betraying him. Betrayal breaks hearts.

Please write verses 12–14, and imagine yourself in the situation. Can you believe that a friend, once close, has insulted and betrayed a love and trust? Ask God to help you with any hurt and pain like this that you may have experienced, as we study this week.

Write out Psalm 55:12–14.

Share your thoughts and feelings about this Scripture.

How could a friendship described as "close fellowship" go horribly wrong?

Something that may have started out so well took a horrible turn; sin entered in and poisoned the friendship.

Dr. Jenn Berman, in a recent radio interview with WebMD, described a toxic friend this way:

> It's someone who, after spending time with them, makes you feel bad about yourself instead of good; someone who tends to be critical of you — sometimes in a subtle way and sometimes not so subtle; a friend who drains you emotionally, financially, or mentally.

For something to become toxic, it has to have something poisonous in it. Listed below are several poisons to friendships. Do you see any of these poisons in your friendships?

Circle any that apply.

Gossip   Jealousy   Control Issues   Neglect

Let's look at God's Word and see what He says about these.

GOSSIP: *"A troublemaker plants seeds of strife; gossip separates the best of friends"* (Proverbs 16:28 NLT).

JEALOUSY: *"For where jealousy and selfish ambition exist, there is disorder and every evil thing"* (James 3:16 NASB).

CONTROLLING: *"One final word of counsel, friends. Keep a sharp eye out for those who take bits and pieces of the teaching that you learned and then use them to make trouble. Give these people a wide berth. They have no intention of living for our Master Christ. They're only in this for what they can get out of it, and aren't above using pious sweet talk to dupe unsuspecting innocents"* (Romans 16:17–18 THE MESSAGE).

NEGLECT: *"But he's already made it plain how to live, what to do, what GOD is looking for in men and women. It's quite simple: Do what is fair and just to your neighbor, be compassionate and loyal in your love, And don't take yourself too seriously—take God seriously"* (Micah 6:8 THE MESSAGE).

We are all sinners; not one of us is perfect, and we have either been hurt or have hurt others by one of those poisons listed above. About nine years ago, poison seeped into one friendship I know about, for a season. That poison manifested itself in various ways. A woman needed help with an event, and because another woman in the friendship wanted the first woman to value her, she volunteered to pick up supplies for the event. This task was simple, but it was a big imposition on the other woman's schedule. Yet she so wanted the woman to like her, and thought if she helped, the woman would see her as important and valuable. It turned out not to be so. In fact, the woman behaved rudely toward the other woman — who had volunteered to help her — and did so in public.

The woman was neglectful and was using the other woman to accomplish her work. She also poisoned the relationship with a grasp for control. However, the other woman who volunteered was looking to a woman for approval and affirmation rather than God, and that is a subtle sin but sin nonetheless.

God tells us, "If we confess our sins, he is faithful and just and will forgive us our sins and purify us from all unrighteousness" (1 John 1:9). That's grace, my friends. We need the gospel every single day. I'm so thankful that Jesus hung on the Cross for our sins and for the sins of our friends.

I pray you will listen to God as you take some time to consider and fully answer the following questions:

What is God saying to me today about some of my relationships?

Has poison seeped into a friendship? If so, what poison(s)?

What do I need to do about it?

God, thank You for never giving up on us. Please continue to reveal to us any friendships that are not glorifying to You. Please strengthen and move us forward in being obedient to what You have placed on our hearts. In Jesus' name, amen.

DAY 2:

DANGEROUS RELATIONSHIPS

When we look at Jesus' life, we see that He had a best friend named John; He was very close to James and Peter; and then He was close to the rest of the Twelve—His disciples—and the 70 followers that He sent out on mission. And He was very close to certain women followers (Luke 8:1–4).

Yet, Jesus always kept as His first priority time with God the Father. Above and beyond everything and everyone else, Jesus made time to commune with Him. Yes, we see Jesus building other spiritual friendships. But Jesus never put His trust and hope in someone or something other than God. This example set by Jesus, when followed, keeps us safe, keeps us on track, and keeps us out of the danger zone.

Martin Luther said, "Whatever your heart clings to and confides in, that is really your God, your functional savior." Our one goal today, as we continue this week in "treacherous ties," is to remain closest to our Savior, and His plan for us, and to keep out of the danger zone. At the end of this day, we should be able to recognize whether our heart is clinging to Jesus or it has crossed over into another area and is clinging to someone else for love and significance.

Let's go back to God's Word, which has a lot to say about the danger zone in both the Old and the New Testament:

"You shall have no other gods before me" (Deuteronomy 5:7).

Do not follow other gods, the gods of the peoples around you (Deuteronomy 6:14).

Jesus said to him, "Away from me, Satan! For it is written: 'Worship the Lord your God, and serve him only'" (Matthew 4:10).

Dear children, keep away from anything that might take God's place in your hearts. (1 John 5:21 NLT).

Therefore, my dear friends, flee from idolatry (1 Corinthians 10:14).

Remember Martin Luther's definition of idolatry: "Whatever your heart clings to and confides in, that is really your God, your functional savior."

A group of people whose hearts and minds focused on something and someone other than God is evident in the instructive biblical account of the Tower of Babel. The issue wasn't simply about the structure they wanted to build; the problem was with the *hearts* of the people and what they were clinging to.

Read Genesis 11:1–9. As we look at God's Word to understand the Tower of Babel, we have to ask how we got from one family that came off the ark, to all of these people populating all of these different regions. That's what the story of the Tower of Babel will answer for us. But to get there, and to see about that danger zone, we have to step back even further—we first have to consider Genesis 10.

Read Genesis 10:1–32. List the names of Noah's three sons.

Noah's three sons settled in three different regions. One with his descendants settled in the Indo-European region (Genesis 10:2–5). Another and his four sons settled in the African/Canaanite regions (vv. 6–20). The other and his descendants settled in the Middle East/Persian regions (Israel, Jordan, and Lebanon).

It's important to note that Genesis 10:8–15 is devoted to a man named Nimrod. Nimrod was *not* a nice man. The Bible says he was "a mighty hunter." The building of the Tower of Babel is credited to Nimrod's reign (Genesis 10:10). And it was Ham's descendants who eventually settled in Babylon under the reign of Nimrod (Genesis 10:20).

In Genesis 9:1, what did God tell Noah and his sons to do? Fill in the blanks: "Then God blessed Noah and his sons, saying to them, 'Be _____ and_____ and _____ the earth.'"

Beginning in Genesis 9:20, we learn a little more about Noah and his children. He was not perfect. After drinking alcohol once, Noah passed out naked. In Noah's fallen condition, his sons revealed something about their hearts. (God is always most concerned about the hearts of His children.)

In your opinion, what does Genesis 9:22 reveal about Ham's heart?

Note the following Scriptures:

"Honor your father and your mother, so that you may live long in the land the LORD your God is giving you" (Exodus 20:12).

"Cursed is anyone who dishonors their father or mother." Then all the people shall say, "Amen!" (Deuteronomy 27:16).

Did Ham honor his father by telling his brothers about his father's naked condition?

Shem and Japheth showed honor to Noah by covering him and protecting him (Genesis 9:23). And when Noah woke up, he found out what Ham had done (v. 24).

Read Genesis 9:24–27. In this passage, Noah blessed Shem's line, which is the line that leads to Jesus Christ. And we learn about Japheth and how his descendants are the Gentiles. These are the people to whom the gospel was preached in the Book of Acts.

With a better understanding of who the sons of Noah were and of what God told them to do, fill in the blanks again:

"Be _____ and _____ and_____ the earth" (Genesis 9:1).

Read Genesis 11:1–4. Ham settled in the land of Shinar.

And then we see God's people clinging to their own plans. They begin to make bricks for building. They decide among themselves to build a city, and decide to build for themselves a tower to reach the heavens. They decide they will "make a name for" themselves — be known. They decide they want to control their destiny and not be scattered over the earth. They act like they are gods who will depend on themselves rather than on Him. They were in the danger zone. Something and someone had taken the place of God.

Read Genesis 11:5–9. How did God respond?

As we close today's study, consider your life and relationships. Consider whether you are in any relationship that is in the danger zone or headed for it. Has someone taken a higher priority in your life than God? We all have "towers" that we are building, brick by brick. Some questions we need to answer include these: Whose building plans am I following?

Is this friendship being built to glorify God?

What is my heart, my intent in regard to the building of this friendship?

Lord God,

We thank You that You are the only Builder who matters. Thank You for sending Your Son from heaven to provide a way for us to become part of Your family so we can dwell in Your house. Thank You for pursuing us when we stray and bringing us back to You.

In Jesus' name, amen.

DAY 3:

BREAKING FREE

*Y*esterday we looked at the Tower of Babel and learned how the hearts of God's people strayed from God. We talked about building friendships with hearts that desire to glorify God and not end up in the danger zone of clinging to someone else in the place of God. Maybe you ended yesterday's study with the Lord pressing on your heart to make changes in a friendship that has become dangerous with pride, people pleasing, control, gossip, jealousy, or neglect.

Can it happen that we are in a place of hearing from God, but the truth is, we just don't want to do what He says? That is called disobedience. This study today encourages us to obey, to have a desire to break free from unhealthy relationships.

About ten years ago, I was wrestling with God about a relationship that did not glorify Him; I did not want to let go. That relationship fed something in me that only God should feed. One day, sitting in my car, I cried out to God: "God, I know this relationship is wrong, but I do not want to give it up! Please, Father, give me the desire to want to give it up. Give me the desire to want to break free and please you." And He did. God—in the way only He can—touched my heart and changed it. He took away the desire I had to cling to someone else and replaced it with a huge desire for only Him. Praise God.

Are you involved in a friendship you cling to more than you cling to Jesus? If so, describe it.

Do you want to break free of relationships that do not glorify God?

At some point in our lives, we all struggle with idols. If that's your situation today, I pray you are stirred with the desire to break free.

Do you need to cry out to God, asking Him to give you the desire to release that unhealthy relationship?

The Gospel of John records a time Jesus asked a man if he wanted to break free from illness. Read the following passage from John 5:

Some time later, Jesus went up to Jerusalem for one of the Jewish festivals. Now there is in Jerusalem near the Sheep Gate a pool, which in Aramaic is called Bethesda and which is surrounded by five covered colonnades. Here a great number of disabled people used to lie — the blind, the lame, the paralyzed. One who was there had been an invalid for thirty-eight years. When Jesus saw him lying there and learned that he had been in this condition for a long time, he asked him, "Do you want to get well?"

"Sir," the invalid replied, "I have no one to help me into the pool when the water is stirred. While I am trying to get in, someone else goes down ahead of me."

Then Jesus said to him, "Get up! Pick up your mat and walk." At once the man was cured; he picked up his mat and walked.

The day on which this took place was a Sabbath (John 5:1–9).

God called one of Karen's friends to Nabukalu, Uganda, almost five years ago. At the time, her calling was to an orphanage with more than 100 orphaned children. She has continued to go yearly, but the calling has changed. Today, her calling is to a village with the purpose of ministering to women and children. Every year, she leaves Uganda humbled and feeling privileged that God would allow her to serve Him with such beautiful and wonderful friends. She writes about a recent visit:

> Last year, our team provided a medical clinic that treated over 2,200 patients. Let's stop right here and point out that I am not a medical person—that's not my gifting! Thankfully, God built an amazing team of doctors and nurses. For many of our friends in Uganda, this was the first time that they had ever seen a doctor. Many said they had been waiting years for a doctor to come to their village. I will forever remember seeing, as our bus approached the village, the faces of those who were literally carrying their loved ones to the clinic. They wanted their loved ones to get well; the loved ones themselves wanted to get well.

Our study for today is about a healing that took place at the pool of Bethesda. Read John 5:1–9 and place yourself in the story. Imagine that you are in Jerusalem when Jesus comes. Maybe you are one of the sick who can't break free of your illness, and you see Jesus walking your way.

Three festivals were held every year in Jerusalem. These festivals, also known as feasts, required all male Jews to attend, which explains why Jesus was there. As you can imagine, any festival requiring all males to attend would cause the population of the community to swell. Many of the Jewish men would bring their families and friends with them.

In John 5:2, we learn of the pool, also known as the house of mercy or house of grace. Many of the sick would stay there for days, whereas others would be brought each day and left at the pool, hoping that day would be the one on which they would be made well.

Some Bible translations do not include verses 3*b* and 4, the part enclosed in brackets below:

Within these lay a large number of the sick—blind, lame, and paralyzed [—waiting for the moving of the water, because an angel would go down into the pool from time to time and stir up the water. Then the first one who got in after the water was stirred up recovered from whatever ailment he had] (John 5:3–4 HCSB).

Reasons for the omission from some translations include the facts that some scholars believe the writing style of these verses does not match John's style and that this text was not in the earliest manuscripts, although it was included in later manuscripts.

While we can't be certain whether the Apostle John or someone else added this text, we do know for certain the pool of Bethesda actually did exist, and a winding, well-worn path outside the gates of the city led to it.

Why do you think the pool of Bethesda was located outside the gates of the city?

When we read about the man who had been sick for 38 years, we may wonder about the person we didn't read about: the loved one who may have carried the man to the pool for 38 years or who may have come to see him and visit with him at the pool. Was that person who carried or ministered to him a parent, a wife, or maybe a best friend? What hope was in the heart of that person for the loved one? How many doctors had they already tried? Yet this man was still not well. How many times might a loved one have said to this man, "Get up. Don't you want to be well?" The waiting continued: one day turned into a month, a month turned into a year, and then year after year passed with no healing.

How do you relate to this story?

Do you identify with the sick man at the pool of Bethesda or with someone desperately wanting a loved one to get well?

Remembering what God has revealed in our hearts regarding our friendships, are you involved in a friendship that has become ill with pride, people pleasing, control, gossip, jealousy, or neglect? Do you want that friendship to be well?

Turn with me to John 4:48 and write the Scripture below:

Now look at John 20:30–31, and write it below:

John 5 shows us not only God's love for His people and His ability to perform miracles, such as healing the physically ill, but also His sovereignty, His timing, and His plan. He is showing us that in *all* things, Jesus Christ is our healer. *He* is our rescue. The man who had been at the pool of Bethesda for 38 years did not know Jesus; Scripture does not show any evidence of his faith before Jesus approached him. The sick man's faith was only in the healing waters; the possibility that Jesus could heal him never entered his mind. Like many persons', this man's expectations of what Jesus could do for him were limited to what he believed was possible.

Consider: which of your friendships might become stronger and healthier?

What would you like Jesus to correct that may be wrong in your friendships, to make them beautiful and right?

From what friendships would you like to break free, and in what friendships do you long for God's healing?

When Jesus asked the invalid man whether he wanted to get well, he responded: "Sir . . . I have no one to help me into the pool when the water is stirred. While I am trying to get in, someone else goes down ahead of me" (John 5:7). Is it time for you to assert different behavior in your friendships?

Are any of the following preventing you from breaking free and getting well? (If so, circle appropriate answers.)

pride   people   pleasing   neglect

control issues   gossip   jealousy

What is God telling you to do? Why do you keep avoiding doing it?

Breaking free, getting well—these require obeying God. "Jesus said to him [the invalid man], 'Get up, take up your bed, and walk.' And at once the man was healed, and he took up his bed and walked" (John 5:8–9 ESV).

Take a few minutes and journal your thoughts from today.

We confess, Lord, that we are sinners, and are sorry for participating in friendships that have become treacherous, and those we have clung to instead of clinging to You. We want to replace sin—that makes relationships unhealthy—with the goodness that comes from Jesus Christ. Thank You, even now, for moving our hearts to please You in our friendships. Please guide us to walk this out. In Jesus' name, amen.

DAY 4:

TRUSTING AGAIN

*W*hat a week! As my friend Karen would say, sweet biscuits and good gravy, I feel like I have been on an emotional roller coaster. That roller coaster has taken me up . . . up . . . up . . . and then has sent me plunging facedown into God's Word. And now, as God wraps His arms around me, comforts me, and smiles at me, I look up to the Father and say, "Let's do it again!" How about you?

Now, I picture us in line at the amusement park again. Our turn is getting closer and closer. I've just turned to you and said, "Well, do you want to do it again? Are we going to trust this roller coaster to bring us safely back, more knowledgeable and stronger for the journey?" Oh my, if we truly believe we have a God who loves us outrageously, who really is for our good, then we should have no hesitation, no lack of trust in Him and His plan for us. Let's go, friends. It's our turn!

Proverbs 3:5 states, "Trust in the LORD with all your heart, and do not rely on your own understanding" (HCSB). Sometimes it's not easy to trust what we don't understand. A lot of times, we desperately want to understand why something has happened before we move forward in trusting. Even as God's beloved children, we're not always given an understanding of circumstances or an explanation as to why things happen the way they do. The Lord God says in Isaiah 55 that His thoughts are not our thoughts and our ways are not His ways. I love how *The Message* gives us the paraphrase of this Scripture:

"I don't think the way you think. The way you work isn't the way I work." God's Decree. "For as the sky soars high above earth, so the way I work surpasses the way you work, and the way I think is beyond the way you think." (Isaiah 55:8–9 THE MESSAGE)

In this Bible study, we have asked God a lot of questions about our faith, our relationships, and our friendships. We've cried out to God our Father wanting to understand why friends have hurt or betrayed us. And we've cried out confessing our own sin of hurting and betraying others. While God never fails to comfort us, He doesn't always answer the question, Why? He is so much greater than we can imagine, and His thoughts are not our thoughts.

Today's lesson on trusting will be from the Book of Philippians, which was written by the Apostle Paul. Read Philippians 4:2–3, then journal write it.

Paul had a great love for the Philippian church, those saints in Christ Jesus at Philippi. The church at Philippi was considered one of the healthiest. Because of Paul's love for this fellowship, he addressed a conflict that needed resolution.

Paul named two women who were involved in a disagreement, Euodia and Syntyche, but he did not share the details of the conflict. We are left to wonder what could have caused such a rift between these two sisters in Christ, who were more than likely very good friends and involved in one of the healthiest churches mentioned in Scripture.

With the omission of the circumstances, we are able to place ourselves in the story.

In the following sentence drawn from Philippians 4:2–3 (HCSB), insert your name in the first blank and the initials of a friend you disagree or disagreed with in the second blank. In the last blank, add the name of your women's ministry director or your small-group leader.

I urge _____ and I urge _____ to agree in the Lord. Yes, I also ask you, _____, to help these women who have contended for the gospel at my side, along with Clement and the rest of my coworkers whose names are in the book of life.

As you think about your friend, can you see how your friendship may have been damaged by pride, control issues, gossip, jealousy, neglect, or a desire to please one another instead of God? In our desire to break free and to be well, God is asking us to trust Him. Trusting God means laying down self, saying it doesn't matter who was right or who was wrong. Trusting God means not looking to place blame, but rather looking at the Cross. Whatever caused the pain in your friendship is sin. And Jesus Christ paid for that sin on the Cross at Calvary. Jesus Christ loves you, and He loves your friend. His desire is to see you trusting God and moving forward. Please read (Romans 10:14–17). Many wonderful online tools are available to help you continue in your study of God's Word. I recommend reading this in *The Message* translation at biblegateway.com. As you search what God's Word says on trusting Him, write down passages that He impresses on your heart.

> *Father God, thank You for loving us so much that You would send Your Son to die for our sins. In our relationships with our friends, remind us that Your Son has already paid that price. An unbelieving world is watching us. May we glorify You as we trust You in our friendships and in our lives. In Jesus' name, amen.*

DAY 5:

MOVING FORWARD

Today's lesson is on moving forward. We will be looking at Joseph's life as a guide in moving forward, noting the treacherous ties he experienced in his life.

Please read Genesis 50:18–21. Joseph had been betrayed by his family and friends. Genesis 50:18–21 is actually the end of the story. In this passage, we see Joseph reassuring his brothers, the very persons who had betrayed him in horrible ways. As Joseph looked on his brothers, I can only imagine the memories running through his mind. These brothers of his caused him pain. Their treachery, their betrayal resulted in young Joseph having to leave his home as a 17-year-old, never to return to that home again.

Genesis 37:23 tells of what happened to that young man: "When Joseph came to his brothers, they stripped off his robe, the robe of many colors that he had on" (Genesis 37:23 HCSB).

Joseph's brothers, out of their hatred and jealousy, tore the coat from his body, threw him into a pit, and then sold him into slavery. But, as we've learned over the last two weeks, many of us have stories of having felt betrayed. God knew before Joseph was born that his brothers would betray him and that he would be sold into slavery and live in Egypt. Remember, our God knows the end from the beginning.

In God's providence, He either causes or allows circumstances to happen that ultimately are for our good and His glory.

What are your thoughts regarding the preceding statement? Is it hard for you to conceive that God might allow difficult things to happen in your friendships?

Looking at your Bible study responses for this week, can you see situations in which difficult and painful circumstances were actually for your good?

In the midst of difficulties, God never leaves us. Oftentimes, the Father will send others to stand beside us during a trial. It could be a new friend or a friend from the past whom God sends to pray, uphold, and point to Jesus.

"Give thanks in all circumstances; for this is God's will for you in Christ Jesus" (1 Thessalonians 5:18). The key to moving forward is thanking God for everything, and that includes the past. Every friend God has allowed into your life has been for a reason. Every circumstance that has been allowed in your friendship has been for your good. Yes, I said every circumstance. I smile even as I type those words because someone somewhere is saying, "You don't know what my friend did to me; you don't know what she said about me." You're right. I don't know, but I know the One who does. I know He loves you with an outrageous love, and He has promised to work all things out for your good and His glory. God deserves hearts of thankfulness and hearts of praise.

Take a few minutes right now to tell God how much you love Him, how thankful you are to be moving forward from difficulties with friends, and, more importantly, how thankful you are for Him.

Every time you cross my mind, I break out in exclamations of thanks to God. Each exclamation is a trigger to prayer. I find myself praying for you with a glad heart. I am so pleased that you have continued on in this with us, believing and proclaiming God's Message, from the day you heard it right up to the present. There has never been the slightest doubt in my mind that the God who started this great work in you would keep at it and bring it to a flourishing finish on the very day Christ Jesus appears. (Philippians 1:3–6 THE MESSAGE)

The Adventure of God's Will

DAY 1:

IN PLACE FOR THE ADVENTURE

*W*e are going to spend our last week talking, studying, and pondering over the adventure of life in Christ. What better passages could we choose to study than the ones about Jesus calling Peter, James, and John to follow Him in His adventure on earth?

Read Luke 5:1–11. Now, before we dive into this Scripture, let's dig into the lives of these fishermen: Peter (also referred to as Simon), James, and John.

Read Matthew 4:18–22. Jesus called these two sets of brothers to follow Him. When we pick up in Luke 5, scholars suggest that the men were keeping close to Jesus but still working as fishermen. Jesus was teaching at the edge of the lake. The crowd was pushing closer to listen. If you've ever attended a conference with open seating, you can imagine this gathering. Except there were no chairs, aisles, or persons with *security* spelled out on their shirts. The people wanted to get closer to Jesus.

In verse 3, Jesus got into one of the boats and did what?

Notice that Simon was washing nets, important business for his livelihood. If the nets were not prepared, they would be unfit to fish with the next day. At Jesus' request, Simon Peter stopped what he was doing, apparently loaded his nets, got in his boat, and put out from the land.

Did Simon Peter hesitate? Not that we know of, but maybe he paused for a moment and considered what he had to do. He had fished all night. I'm sure he was tired, and he still had to clean and mend his nets. But he set aside his plans to do Jesus' bidding.

What if Jesus called you today and said, "Let's go; I have something for us to do together"? Would you say yes even if you were tired and working on a deadline?

Simon Peter was in his comfort zone—fishing. He was doing what came naturally to him when Jesus called him to set it aside for a time. Is the Lord calling you to something inconvenient? Maybe He is asking you to do something that just doesn't work for your schedule.

I know what that feels like. I've been there, and as I complete this study, I'm in the midst of these very circumstances. I'm busy with work and family. I have so much going on that setting it all aside to write this Bible study has been a challenge—but it has also been one of the biggest blessings of my life. I'm blown away by how God has given me the words to write. In my weakness, He is so strong.

Write out Philippians 4:13:

What can we do in Christ?

What is God calling you to do today?

Simon Peter's first step was to get in the boat; that was an easy one for him. Maybe God is asking you to do something within your comfort zone. Sometimes I think we expect God's calling to be *huge* and accompanied by flashing lights and dinging bells. That's not always the case. Sometimes the adventure begins with the familiar.

Lord, today I'm asking that You reveal Your next step to us. Lord, we're not asking for the entire plan because that's not ours to know; we are just asking for affirmation of the next step. Lord, make Your calling clear to us. Let us know that we are on the right path. Lord, I ask that You show each of us Your strength in our weaknesses. Lord, I ask that You show us Your glory! God, we want more of You! Amen.

DAY 2:

WILLING TO GO

I'm always ready for the adventure—until it's time to leave, that is. When that time comes, I have a hundred reasons why I can't go right then. Work, family, friends, social obligations, church—you name the excuse, I'll use it. The point is not that I don't *want* the adventure; it's that often the reality doesn't match up with my expectation. I love the getting ready part—the planning, talking, and figuring out what to take on the adventure. But when the time comes to leave, I get butterflies and begin to wonder, *Is this the right thing to do?*

A couple of years ago, my friend Melinda and I were talking about our love for all things vintage. I came up with a brilliant idea: Let's buy an old Airstream trailer and travel old Route 66 across America.

Now, if you don't know about Route 66, let me enlighten you a bit. Route 66 was known as the Mother Road, and it stretched from Chicago to Los Angeles. The road was the main thoroughfare for travelers, and the highway was filled with iconic billboards, unique motels, and kitschy roadside attractions. Entire towns and businesses were built around Route 66. Sadly, the development of the interstate system made Route 66 a thing of the past, and it was officially decommissioned in the 1980s.

Just because the road no longer shows up on the official maps doesn't make people love it any less. The towns are quieter, the billboards are faded, and many of the roadside attractions sit empty. But people still travel the old route looking to relive those days gone by. This is exactly what Melinda and I planned to do with our yet-to-be purchased Airstream trailer.

The whole plan seemed like a wonderful idea until we both realized we lacked two very important skills: (1) driving while pulling a trailer and (2) backing up with a trailer attached to a vehicle. So we considered our options: (1) get a small trailer and (2) drive only forward.

After careful consideration, we realized that the inability to back up could severely hamper our adventure. We considered canceling the whole idea, but it quickly became evident that God was up to something—and that something would happen out on old Route 66. While we were more than willing to go, we just didn't see it working well for us. We are two Southern girls—one from Texas and one from Alabama—who know little about the West. We say y'all a lot and talk with a drawl. What would we have for individuals we met out on the road? Still, like Simon Peter, we just did as the Lord asked, and we pushed off from the shore and trusted Jesus had a plan for us.

Read Luke 5:1–11 again. (And let me say, you will likely know this passage by heart at the end of this week!) Yesterday we discussed Simon setting out in his boat at Jesus' request. Today we're going to focus on verses 4 and 5.

What did Jesus tell Simon Peter to do in verse 4?

This sounds like a normal request to us. Yet this request was anything but normal. According to biblical scholars, putting nets into the deep was a futile effort, and every fisherman at that lake knew it. But let's see how Simon Peter handles the directive from Jesus.

What did Simon Peter say to Jesus about the fishing (v. 5)?

What did Simon say that he would do (v. 5)?

I love that beginning phrase. I want it to be my phrase for this year and beyond: "At Your word, Lord." When God calls us to this adventure of faith, He is not calling us to the normal, usual, or average. He is calling us to the supernatural. Now, don't think I'm talking about mystics or that chick on reality TV who talks with dead persons. I'm not. I'm talking about the God of the universe sharing with us His power. He is not of this world—and His power is beyond anything we can even begin to imagine. Read the following Scriptures, and write by each reference something that passage reveals about God's power:

Matthew 17:20

John 11:43–44

Ephesians 1:20

God's power can move mountains and raise the dead. It can save a sinner like me. He called me, a person unworthy to even say His holy name, to Himself. He uses me for His work; this is the *most* supernatural thing I've ever known.

Simon Peter knew no fish would likely be caught out in the deep. He was a professional fisherman. He knew those waters, but he also knew there was something special about this Jesus. Simon Peter did as Jesus asked; he took his boat to the deep and tossed his net out into the water.

Sometimes God calls us to do something that goes against our training and knowledge. When the Lord called Melinda and me to head out for a trip on Route 66, we originally thought it was all about fun and adventure. We quickly saw evidence that God had more planned. He gave us a vision of girlfriend gatherings along the road. We set up several live Internet gatherings and invited women across the country to join us as we experienced God in a fun and fresh way. We had many meltdowns and "we can't do this" fits, but we moved forward with an "At Your word, Lord" attitude. We didn't feel equipped or able, but God had His plan in motion.

Is God calling you to go against the grain, like Simon Peter did when he tossed the net into the deep water? If so, I encourage you to pray your way through. I promise you that Karen, Melinda, and I are praying for you.

In closing today, I leave you with two passages of Scripture to read, please: Ephesians 2:1–10 and 3:16–21. Once you've read these, pray through what the Lord is telling you.

How is the Lord leading you?

Tell Him you are willing and ready to go on this adventure in faith!

Dear Lord,

I pray Your blessing over each of us. Lord, point us in the direction You have for us. You alone are the One we worship. It's only in You and through You that we have access to power. Lord, show Yourself to us in a mighty way. Amen.

DAY 3:

NOT JUST YOU

I want to tell you more about that Route 66 adventure story today. I'm so cautious to not leave a friend out (because I know just what that feels like), so Melinda and I invited Karen to join us out on the road. But Karen just couldn't make it happen.

When Melinda and I hit the road, we had a color-coded chart with all our stops, motels, daily mileage, and the live-feed girlfriend gatherings noted. We were excited to set out on the adventure, and we had a great handle on the sightseeing. But we were very fuzzy on the girlfriend gatherings. We didn't quite know how they would work; we just knew that God had a plan.

An Inconvenient Plan

Please read Luke 5:2.

What were the fishermen doing?

This net Simon tossed into the lake was the very one he had spent time cleaning and mending. To throw it out again meant he would have to start that cleaning process all over again, but throw it out into the water again he did.

Read Luke 5:6–7. What kind of catch did they have?

How many boats did they fill with fish?

This story reminds me that responding to Jesus' call on my life is important not only for me, but also for other persons in my life. What if Simon Peter had said, "No, thanks," to Jesus when Jesus told him to put his nets into the deep? What if he'd explained to Jesus that he'd cleaned his nets and really didn't have the time to clean them again?

Of course, Simon Peter's life would have been very different, but what about the lives of those around him? This passage names James and John, but other persons were on that shore watching. Jesus targeted the hearts of the fishermen and showed them His glory. He blessed them their livelihood as well. This catch meant they could provide for their families. When Simon said yes to an inconvenient plan, he and all those around him were greatly blessed.

A Roadside Gathering

When Melinda and I planned our first girlfriend gathering, we didn't have much more set up than just a place: Wigwam Motel in Holbrook, Arizona. The place could be described as a kitschy roadside. The entire motel consisted of 18 individual concrete tepees. It was fun and unusual. But the gathering part—now that's a different story.

We forgot to consider that Wi-Fi might not be available everywhere, and doing a live-feed event, as you probably know, requires some type of Internet connection. After much panic, we found ourselves outside our personal wigwam with the laptop sitting on the roof of a vintage, rusted-out 1938 Hudson. It wasn't quite as we'd planned, and it certainly wasn't convenient, but it was a blessing. We talked with women around the country, we shared an amazing Arizona sunset, and we were all greatly blessed.

While our gathering on Route 66 does not compare with the incredible miracle that Simon Peter experienced, we share one thing with him—a heart that said, *at Your word, Lord.*

What is your heart saying today? Is God calling you out of the convenient? Are you willing?

Today, please write your prayer. Ask God where He's calling you today, and your response.

DAY 4:

THE HEART OF WORSHIP

song entitled, "Live Like That," performed by one of my favorite bands, Sidewalk Prophets, gives me chills every time I hear it. If you take the time to locate it and listen to it, I think you will be greatly blessed. David Frey, Ben McDonald, and Ben Glover give us lyrics that include this snippet reframed here: "Was I Jesus to the least of those . . . I want to live . . . so that everything I say and do points to You." I'm blessed to know these guys and work alongside them in my everyday job. (I work in the Christian entertainment and travel industry.)

I want people to know who Jesus is through me. I wish that meant I live every day as a shining example of Christian love, but it doesn't. I fail—but with every failing, I pull myself up and ask God to work in my life. Where are you today in your "Live Like That" life? Does your life point people to Jesus? Rank yourself from 1 (no one knows I know Jesus) to 10 (It is obvious that I follow Jesus Christ.).

Facedown in Worship

When we closed yesterday, Simon Peter had tossed his clean net into the deep waters after explaining to Jesus that he'd fished all night and not caught anything. He and his companions pulled up enough fish to fill two boats to their capacity.

Read Luke 5:8–9. What did Simon Peter do when he saw the catch that was hauled into the boats?

Why do you think he did this?

Simon Peter had witnessed Jesus teaching and performing miracles, but this simple act of filling his boat with fish drove Simon Peter to his knees.

Do you think Simon was overcome because Jesus cared about him personally? Jesus came to Simon Peter's comfortable place—the water—and showed He cared for Peter. Jesus reached out to him and blessed his work as a fisherman.

Jesus operates in the personal realm, as well as in the big picture. He cares about the details in our lives.

Read Colossians 1:15–17. What is Christ referred to as in verse 15?

What was created by Him (v. 16)?

Write out verse 17 in the space provided.

This passage describes Jesus, the Son of God, the Christ who told Simon Peter to cast his net into the deep, the Christ who wants to shine in you and through you.

Going On

Even in the presence of the awesome power available through Jesus, we have no need to feel guilt or fear.

Read Luke 5:8–11. What did Jesus tell Simon in verse 10?

Don't you love this? How often have you felt overwhelmed when tackling something? Isn't it wonderful when you feel the Holy Spirit come over you with a sense of great peace?

It has been a rough season, but God has poured His peace over me. When my Dad passed away weeks before my deadline, God kept giving me peace. Again and again, I heard Jesus' words: "Don't be afraid" (v. 10). I trusted His plan.

Simon Peter's actions tell us that he trusted Jesus' plan too. In verse 11, Simon and his partners, James and John, pulled their boats onto the shore and left everything to follow Him.

Are you willing to take that step and follow Jesus like you've never followed Him before?

> *Lord,*
>
> *What a journey we've been on. I want to have a willing heart to step out in faith. Help me trust Your plan, even when I don't understand it. Lord, let me see Your glory, even though I don't deserve it. Lord, let me serve Your people as an offering of worship to You. When people see me, let them see only You. Lord, I love You so. Amen.*

DAY 5:

Follow Him

It's been an amazing journey through faith, friendships, and relationships. We still have today and then my girlfriends pulled together a wonderful devotional journey for you.

Looking Back

Let's take a look back at each week we've been through and review what God has been saying to us. Review each week's material: review your notations, journals—answers you gave, things you highlighted, Scriptures you noted—and recall what the Lord showed you with these three basic questions:

What is one thing that stands out to me about this week?

What did the Lord teach me through the week of study?

How am I applying the lessons learned to everyday life?

As you read again Luke 5:11, what three things did the men do?

Why? Jesus called them to follow Him—that's why. They walked away from everything to receive the best thing—Jesus. We have that same call to follow Him. He is calling us away from everything worldly to the best thing—Himself.

Looking Forward

These last six weeks, we've been working toward an authentic faith, and that authentic faith is all about Jesus. He is the reason we walk in faith. He is our faith. Be who He says you are.

> *Walk in truth.*
> *Walk in love.*
> *Walk with friends.*
> *Walk with Him!*

As we close today, I want to pray a Scripture over you.

> *Father God, I am so honored to have been with these women through Your Word as we've walked closer to You and practiced authentic faith. Lord, thank You for this tiny sliver of time with these precious women. I pray that I'll get to meet many of them this side of heaven. Jesus, thank You for being You! Your glory is breathtaking. Amen.*

My goal is that they may be encouraged in heart and united in love, so that they may have the full riches of complete understanding, in order that they may know the mystery of God, namely, Christ, in whom are hidden all the treasures of wisdom and knowledge (Colossians 2:2–3).

Diving Deeper Devotionals

What's next? With the collaboration of my friends Karen and Melinda, this will guide you through devotions connected to this study! Work at your own pace or your girlfriends group's pace.

Around the Next Corner

You've read the book. You've dug deep in the Word with your girlfriends and considered what authenticity in faith and relationships really looks like. But now what? Do you just pack up what you learned and put it on the shelf with the book, and wait for the next Bible study?

I sure hope not.

Bible studies are supposed to translate into real-life change. Instead of sitting in a class and giving back what you've learned in a test form, you're supposed to give your Bible study knowledge back to the world, pouring out what you've been given to facilitate change. This is where the devotional part of the study comes in.

It takes weeks to make a habit, I have heard. So we've got four weeks of personal form devotionals for each of you to consider (five each week), and then some weekly connection ideas that will help you and your study girls continue the practice of meeting together regularly. Each week, we'll touch on the following five different areas of authenticity:

- Real Me
- Real Grace
- Real Fellowship
- Real Friendship
- Real Faith

It is our hope that these devotionals will help us walk out what we've learned and be those world changers we so long to be.

God—He's always around the next corner. And because of Him, we can all relax and enjoy the journey.

God has provided for us through His Son Jesus the grandest adventure of all.

WEEK 1   DAY 1: REAL ME

Melinda knows from personal experience that jet lag is a real thing.

> After a wonderful anniversary trip, my husband and I got home late, and fell into bed, but jet lag kept us awake at 4:00 A.M. In addition to too little sleep, I was battling a bug that I'd picked up.
>
> I called my doctor's office. Arriving there, I settled into the waiting room, watching some children's programming.
>
> Then I heard an announcement: "Miss Robinson, will you please come to the window?" I calmly threw my purse over my shoulder and obeyed the request, as did another woman. Suddenly, I realized what had happened. My maiden name is Robinson, but I have not been Miss Robinson in decades. I hurried back to my seat.
>
> Later, I thought about it. Don't we have a tendency to do this? To slip back into our old lives and habits when suddenly something triggers a response that pulls us right back to where we were. This happens even though we may have been away from that place for a *long* time. This is why we're supposed to be on the lookout and guard our hearts. We can get worn down and careless with our vigilance, and that's just when an enemy who longs to see us fall calls to us with an old name.
>
> I'm pleased to say that, after some rest, the next day and the ones following found me more alert and able to remember my name . . . my forever name . . . *Redeemed.*

- *Therefore, if anyone is in Christ, he is a new creation. The old has passed away; behold, the new has come* (2 Corinthians 5:17 ESV).
- *Other Scriptures to consider:* Isaiah 56:5; Ephesians 4:22–24; Proverbs 4:23–27; 1 Peter 5:8

QUESTIONS TO PONDER
- Satan uses lies—names—such as **worthless, stupid,** and others, to try to hold us hostage. These are often covered over with something we've manufactured so people will never know what we've accepted as the truth about ourselves. What is an old name to which you are especially susceptible?
- Christ immediately wipes out the old names when we accept the gift of salvation. Every other old label becomes **Redeemed**. Sometimes, though, we choose to stay right where we were. How can it affect the authenticity of our friendships if we are still operating in the lies of the old, instead of the truth of the new?

WEEKLY CONNECTION IDEA
Meet for coffee, and draw names of the group members. Give the person you drew a new, affirming name, and tell that person why you chose it. Build each other up.

WEEK 1   DAY 2: REAL GRACE
Recently, I had an interesting conversation with a friend of mine. She has kind of a tough exterior, having come through some pretty hard knocks in her life, and she is uncomfortable when people see glimpses of her soft side. But trust me when I say she's a *softy*.

When I told her I'd been on to her softy ways from almost the beginning, she said she reserves the side of herself that showcases her kindness and compassion for her immediate family and the few persons she really cares about—nobody else. She was quick to add her reason for this: She's found that most don't deserve it. And, hey, why waste the energy?

How easy it is to feel that way. So many persons don't return the kindness. After expending all that energy to administer kindness without receiving anything back, motivation to keep it up is hard to maintain. We are a self-preserving society, after all, and we put looking out for number one pretty high on the priority list. But here's the deal: Jesus tells us to do exactly the opposite:

- Pray for your enemies.
- Treat others like you want to be treated.
- Love one another.

And, why should we do these things? Because Jesus did. He prayed for, treated well, and loved the dregs of society, the shunned and unclean outside the city gate, the hated tax collectors, the very persons who had nailed Him to the Cross . . . *while He was hanging on it*!

I don't believe all those commands were handed down just for the sake of commanding. No. I believe Jesus told us to do those things because they make us *more*. They expand our eyes to look beyond what we see. They expand our minds to think beyond ourselves. They expand our hearts to love beyond what we ever thought possible and free us up to experience all this in a new way.

I don't know about you, but I think becoming more of a person is worth the extra energy because, in the process, I'm becoming more like Jesus.

He didn't start this whole love ball rolling because we deserved it. He started it because *not a one of us did*.

- *"But I tell you, love your enemies and pray for those who persecute you"* (Matthew 5:44).
- *Read also:* Matthew 7:12; Luke 23:34; John 13:34; Romans 5:8

QUESTIONS TO PONDER
- When you consider how you feel when grace is extended to you, how does your perspective on offering grace change?
- How does the fact that no one deserves grace (including you and me) impact the way you approach your relationships?

WEEK 1   DAY 3: REAL FELLOWSHIP

While it's true that we love technology and social media and have met some friends through it, those friendships are "best" when we've brought them out of the computer and into real life. Certainly, our love for friends in the online world is *real*, but, in reality, relationship with most of them is *virtual*. How is it that virtual friends can receive much more of our time than the ones in real life?

If you find yourself caught in one world, blinded to and no longer stepping foot into the other, maybe it's time to evaluate the real scoop on virtual living. Social media can be used to God's glory, but there comes a time when you need to turn off the technology and do life in the real world.

Maybe you could call a neighbor—soon. Maybe she's got a fresh pot of coffee just waiting.

- *And let us not neglect our meeting together, as some people do, but encourage one another, especially now that the day of his return is drawing near* (Hebrews 10:25 NLT).
- *Read also:* Proverbs 4:25; Romans 14:19

QUESTIONS TO PONDER
- After close consideration, is technology use causing you to live more of your life virtually than you realized?
- Think of two persons in your real, everyday life with whom you've lost contact and make arrangements to spend some time with them, face-to-face. Sacrifice technology time to do it.

WEEKLY CONNECTION IDEA
Decide as a group an amount of time each of you will sacrifice from your social media time, and hold each other accountable. Determine how to use that time as a group to benefit the community.

WEEK 1   DAY 4: REAL FRIENDSHIP
Little children need grown-ups in their lives to spot the danger for them as they travel down life's road. We're really no different. When was the last time you thanked someone for telling you something you should've noticed yourself?

I think we do offer our thanks for simple things like someone reminding us of our car keys when we leave them at the grocery checkout or someone pointing out a tire going flat. But I'm talking about stuff that's really important: like when we are going down a wrong life path or getting too close in a relationship that is not good for us. In those instances, we are blinded by the circumstance itself and often don't see the red flags and warning signs until it's too late. Do you have someone around you who would step up and tell you that you're headed in a wrong direction? Moreover, would you welcome that person's input and offer thanks for it?

I'm grateful to have a husband who will do this, but I also have couple of girlfriends to whom I've given permission to yank me aside and tear my blinders off so I can actually see what's happening. It's no fun to experience, but in that somber moment of realization of indisputable truth, I can finally look up and receive it.

If you don't have any "spotters" in your life, why not recruit a couple for yourself? Give them permission to call you out when you need it. I promise it'll only sting a little because, it'll all be done in the name of love.

- *Instead, speaking the truth in love, we will grow to become in every respect the mature body of him who is the head, that is, Christ* (Ephesians 4:15).
- *Read also:* Luke 17:3–4; Galatians 6:1–3

QUESTIONS TO PONDER
- How does trusting others to keep you accountable encourage you to be more honest with yourself?
- What are benefits to the friendship, itself, when permission to speak truth into each other's life is given?

WEEK 1   DAY 5: REAL FAITH

We have no time for the unexpected, and yet, it happens. Sometimes, sudden interruptions in our lives can feel like a sucker punch. Certainly, an unexpected flu can knock you back, but what about the *real* body blows: the diagnosis of major illness, the revelation of an affair, a sudden layoff, or news of an addicted child? These blows knock the air right out of you and leave you feeling dead.

The initial response to the blow may be the assumption that God has left the building. How could this happen? *Why* did this happen? *And where in the world is God?*

However, after the initial pain of the punch has subsided and you've recovered the air that was knocked out of you, you realize that God didn't leave at all; you were just thrown away from Him by the force of the blow. The rubber of your faith has just met the road, and it's up to you to decide whether you're willing to walk back to Him. I'm here to tell you that, if you dare to walk back, you'll find out that this slam of the unexpected can be an extraordinary gift of faith building. If you dare to put the pain in His hands and let Him do whatever He sees fit with it (regardless of what you think the outcome should be), you will experience the love, the power, the freedom of God in a way you never have—in a way you never thought possible. You'll watch as your faith solidifies into something unshakable, and the next time a left hook comes flying your way, it won't knock you quite as far.

I won't go so far as to say that I welcome life's punches. However, I am thankful that it's possible to make it through the challenges, not only with your faith intact, but with a strength of faith newly discovered, deepening every time we get up from a blow and dare to walk back to His arms, every time we dare to trust the One who is never taken by surprise.

- *Desperate, I throw myself on you: you are my God! Hour by hour I place my days in your hand, safe from the hands out to get me. Warm me, your servant, with a smile; save me because you love me* (Psalm 31:14–16 THE MESSAGE).
- *Read also:* Isaiah 43:2; Nahum 1:7; Romans 8:29–30

QUESTIONS TO PONDER
- Consider the best times of your life and the worst. In which did you see the biggest measure of personal growth and growth in your faith?
- How have these times of growth better prepared you for the next "sucker punch"?

WEEK 2   DAY 1: REAL ME

Once, when I was visiting my daughter's family in Florida, I made an appointment with the hairdresser I had when I had lived in the area. On the day of the appointment, I told my granddaughter, Lilli, where I was heading. When she learned she wasn't going with me, she wasn't at all pleased. According to my daughter, a short while after I left, Lilli took her blanket and posse of bedtime pals and announced that she didn't feel well. When asked what was wrong, she simply stated, "Only Mimmie understands me."

Oh *my*. I won't be praying her into a sparkling Hollywood career anytime soon, but if the good Lord decides that's going to be her path anyway, the movie people won't be getting anyone short on dramatic talent when they get her.

Isn't it interesting that, even at two years old, we long for others to understand us? It seems we are born *needing* to be understood completely for who we are. All through our lives, we move from person to person to find that understanding because absolutely no one—not our parents, not our spouses, not our best friends—really understands the *all* of us.

I might have a pretty good handle on what makes Lilli tick right now, but most likely a time will come when she will completely baffle me (teen years, anyone?), and she will have to rethink her bold claim. I think that's because, as we grow, we start to become less and less honest about our feelings. We bottle things up, we self-protect, we put on a brave face, and we let others see less of our real selves. We get so good at it that we begin to hide things even from ourselves.

Only one being fully understands us, only one really, truly *knows* our thoughts, feelings, and hearts: God alone. We can't hide from Him, even though we've all tried at one time or another.

—MELINDA GARMAN

I'm so grateful that when other persons close to me seem to fall short in this understanding department, I have Someone who offers *real understanding*, Someone in whom I can rest so I can cease my running. Blanket and stuffed animals are optional.

- *You know me inside and out* (Psalm 139:15 THE MESSAGE).
- *Read also:* Psalm 139:1–18; Romans 5:8

QUESTIONS TO PONDER
- In whom have you tried to find complete understanding as a person?
- How has placing expectations for understanding on other persons had an impact on your relationships? Your friendships?

WEEK 2   DAY 2: REAL GRACE

The day before Kevin's sister's wedding, he and I were standing under the trees where the ceremony was to take place. I stood on a big, flat stone where she would stand, with her daughter, looking at her groom. I said, "This is a literal step in the right direction for your sister. She will step off of this into a beautiful new beginning."

Call me a romantic, but I think we need to take stock of things like this. It's like a declaration of a work God has done. It's noticing it and being grateful for His grace in our lives.

And this was not just any work—this was His specialty: the fresh start, the do-over, the *do-better*.

The thing I love is that God is not just offering occasional second chances. Every day is a new beginning. We get to start again every time we slip up and fall back into an old habit that's not that good for us, or hurt those around us out of fear, or walk away from God Himself. Some consequences to work through may remain (sin typically leaves a mess to clean up somewhere), but the humble heart that kneels at the foot of God gets a do-over every time.

If you think your yesterdays are simply too much or too heavy or too messy for God, I say, "Give Him a try." He's a lot bigger than you think and a lot more forgiving. Plus, how can giving God a shot at the cleanup be any worse than living in the mess and devastation that sin has left behind?

It was a beautiful wedding, by the way. And do you know what? A wedding of our own—a wedding in heaven—is being planned for every one of us who trusts God for second chances in this life. A feast and celebration will take place in which the Groom and His bride (that's us, the church!). will stand possibly on a stone, gratefully marking that day of new beginnings (God's specialty) by stepping off into our eternity—our very own step in the right direction.

—MELINDA GARMAN

- *Then if my people who are called by my name will humble themselves and pray and seek my face and turn from their wicked ways, I will hear from heaven and will forgive their sins and restore their land* (2 Chronicles 7:14 NLT).
- *Read also:* John 3:16–17; Revelation 19:6–9

QUESTIONS TO PONDER
- How does the continual gift of God's grace change the way you live?
- How does it change the way you give back to the world?

WEEK 2   DAY 3: REAL FELLOWSHIP
I read recently about an old teen organization that was started by the YWCA prior to World War I called "Girl Reserves." It was "dedicated to improving relationships between female students" and hosted lectures on such topics as popularity versus success and gossip versus conversation. Their pledge went like this:

As a Girl Reserve,
I will try
To face life squarely,
To find and give the best.
I will try to be

Gracious in manner
Impartial in judgment
Ready for service
Loyal to friends

Reaching toward the best
Earnest in purpose
Seeing the beautiful
Eager for knowledge
Reverent to God
Victorious over self
Ever dependable
Sincere at all times

Almost 100 years later, this is still an excellent pledge to adopt, even as adult women—maybe especially so in that case! I'm thinking that old high school lunchroom etiquette needs an overhaul. The evil one who wrote it is no Emily Post. I say we recite our pledge and push our lunch tables together, learn a few moves from the girls in chess club, perfect the way we say, *Je t'aime petite amie* with the French club, and join our voices in praise with the music department. And who *knows* what all we'll gain from letting the ones from the far reaches join the group?

Join me for lunch, won't you? Let's find out.

- *The way God designed our bodies is a model for understanding our lives together as a church: every part dependent on every other part, the parts we mention and the parts we don't, the parts we see and the parts we don't. If one part hurts, every other part is involved in the hurt, and in the healing. If one part flourishes, every other part enters into the exuberance. You are Christ's body—that's who you are! You must never forget this. Only as you accept your part of that body does your "part" mean anything* (1 Corinthians 12: 25–27 THE MESSAGE).
- *Read also:* 1 Corinthians 12:12–13

QUESTIONS TO PONDER

- Think about your experiences in high school, and then any experience as an adult in which you've felt excluded. How are these feelings contradictory to what you've come to understand about real fellowship?
- Think of a time when you've felt welcomed and included. How does this showcase the concept of all being part of the body of Christ?

Plan a fun social gathering of your group at someone's home, and have each person invite an unbelieving friend. Welcome, love, and accept everyone who comes. Be the body of Christ to them, and encourage them to pray to become a part.

WEEK 2   DAY 4: REAL FRIENDSHIP

Ants move in a frenetic way, hundreds marching back and forth, to and fro. How can they carry loads so much heavier than what they actually weigh, and fellow ants help one another carry their loads, and keep moving toward the destination?

All around us are persons who have been crushed under the weight of their burdens. We are only human, after all. We tire out and become weak. The burdens become too much to carry. Unless someone comes along and carries them for us for a while, we might just stop dead in our tracks, faith in the dust, and not move another inch. I'm grateful that we have the power to relieve those persons of a burden or three by carrying them on to their destination—to the very feet of the only One who has control over any of it. I'm also grateful we have the power to do this for others because *I* might be the one needing help on the road one day.

Prayer helps lift loads. It's the leverage that makes carrying such heavy weight possible. Whose burdens can you bear today, or to whom can you reach out if you are the one whose faith is down in the dirt? Together, we can pull it out and brush it off. Together we can give those burdens the ol' heave-ho.

- *Carry each other's burdens, and in this way you will fulfill the law of Christ* (Galatians 6:2).
- *Read also:* Ecclesiastes 4:9; Matthew 18:19–20

QUESTIONS TO PONDER
- We've all had friends do nice things for us during the easy and happy times of our lives. Fewer and more precious are the times when others have come alongside to help us carry our heaviest burdens. Remember a time when you've been given this gift. How did your view of that friendship change?

- How do acts like this factor into what you've come to know as real friendship?

WEEKLY CONNECTION IDEA

Select a woman within your group or a single mom in your church who is struggling, and work together as a group to creatively bless her and meet some of her needs.

WEEK 2   DAY 5: REAL FAITH

WEEK 3   DAY 1: REAL ME

WEEK 3   DAY 2: REAL GRACE

WEEK 3   DAY 3: REAL FELLOWSHIP

At a well-stocked bird feeder, you'll see variances in birds' color, size, and pattern. But for all their differences, they have one thing in common. In cold weather, almost every bird puffs out its feathers completely. With feathers sticking straight out, birds look twice their size. But we all know that underneath, these are still tiny, hollow-boned creatures that don't weigh much more than the feathers they wear.

Birds and people are not that different when it comes to keeping out the cold. We puff ourselves up against it and try to appear bold and big, as though there is nothing we can't face. Life's frigid air seeps in relentlessly, but we stoically put on a show that we are handling it all. The truth, however, is found underneath, where our brokenness and hurting hearts feel barely protected by our own hollow-feeling bones.

Recently, I saw one of those birds—a very small finch—do something I'd never seen before. A cardinal was perched on a lower, more interior branch of a tree; it had found a place near the trunk that was sturdier in the wind. That little finch settled on the same branch and shimmied right up next to that cardinal. Once the finch was close, it seemed to relax its feathers a little, returning to almost its normal size. The cardinal never made a move to chase it off; they just sat together quietly, side by side.

You know, I think that little finch was on to something. We don't have to pretend we're OK when we're not. We can find a friend who is on a sturdier branch and let that friend shield us from the cold for a while. Right there, we can let down our guard and just be.

It turns out that the cold deep inside is easier to eradicate when there isn't a puffed-up show of feathers in the way. Just ask the birds.

- *"And as you wish that others would do to you, do so to them"* (Luke 6:31 ESV).
- *Read:* Psalm 17:8, Psalm 91:1–2

QUESTIONS TO PONDER
So often we view fellowship in a social way, a gathering of friends or like-minded persons having a lively exchange of thoughts. Sometimes, though, real fellowship doesn't require any words at all, just the act of being there with another human being—a simple, yet profound, show of solidarity. Can you think of a time when you experienced this type of fellowship?

Think of someone in your Bible study group or in your everyday life who could use a simple show of support. Will you demonstrate your support for that person—not try to fix the problem, but just be there with them as they weather it?

WEEK 3   DAY 4: REAL FRIENDSHIP
Recently, Melinda had the opportunity to show some of her favorite parts of Texas to her sweet Iowan friend, Lynne. With a full heart, she dropped Lynne at the airport and made the familiar

journey back home—back from an incredible week, back from some great time for the soul.

As I drove, I thought about the conversations that we'd had and realized that we had talked nonstop the entire time. It's true that we don't get to see each other very often, and we *are* girlfriends, among whom chattiness seems a given. But the interesting thing is this: Lynne and I are both born listeners. People naturally talk to us, sharing with us their joys and sorrows. We were created to listen, and we listen with pleasure. While listeners encourage talking and get the ball rolling, they typically sit back once that's done and start taking it all in. They don't usually talk much more themselves.

During our trip, however, that just wasn't the case. This was an interesting realization that I tucked away for further pondering.

I eventually pulled into my drive, my heart swelling at the sight of my home. Oh, how I love it. When I started to get ready for bed, the thought occurred to me, *What a gift listening is.* Even when we're listeners, we need a safe place to talk, just like anyone else. Certainly, we can go to God at any time to spill our souls, but when another human being whom we trust and love affords us that gift, it's a unique and wonderful blessing.

If you have a born listener in your life, give that person the same gift back. It will be treasured beyond anything else you can give. And if you *are* the born listener, find that person who will let you spill your soul and go for it. Be the one to give the gift to yourself.

Trust me; you'll be the better—and the *lighter*—for it.

- *"He who has an ear, let him hear"* (Revelation 2:7 ESV).
- *Read:* Proverbs 1: 5, 33 and 2:2-5; *Mark 7:14*

QUESTIONS TO PONDER
- Are you a born listener or are you more comfortable talking?

- Everyone wants to know that what they say is being valued, especially among friends. How does the gift of listening, giving your full attention to another, separate acquaintances from real friends? How does this build authenticity?

WEEKLY CONNECTION IDEA

Have a potluck dinner for your group at someone's home. Using some thought-provoking icebreaker questions (examples below), give the less talkative girls in your group the opportunity to answer each of the questions first. Let the most talkative give them the gift of listening.

- What three words would you like your best friends to use to describe you, and why?
- What two qualities do you value in your closest friends, and why?
- What is one fear that you have?
- If you could ask God one question, and you knew He would answer right away, what would you ask?
- When did God become more than a word to you? How did it happen?

WEEK 3   DAY 5: REAL FAITH

There is a basic illustration of an age-old concept, but it came to mind recently when I received bad news from three different persons. Those three struggling persons, thankfully, are all wise. They've built their houses—their lives—on the Rock. But that doesn't mean they don't feel the howling wind and driving rain beating against them when it starts to storm. Their news, all different, ran the gamut: from a young life taken by a suicide no one saw coming, to sudden job loss, to a cancer diagnosis after a routine physical. All were storms brewing just outside the scope of view on their radars, but not one—*not even one*—was outside the scope of God's view. With their lives built on Him, the One who saw those storms coming, they don't have to worry about weathering the storm. They just have to be concerned with clinging to the Rock as the storm rages, knowing their foundation isn't going anywhere. And that right there provides *a lot* of hope.

I know that my friends, though knocked around and probably battered and bruised, will still be standing, too, when their storms finally quiet down.

Surviving a storm is all about your foundation. We've got to build on a solid foundation.

- *"Therefore everyone who hears these words of mine and puts them into practice is like a wise man who built his house on the rock. The rain came down, the streams rose, and the winds blew and beat against that house; yet it did not fall, because it had its foundation on the rock. But everyone who hears these words of mine and does not put them into practice is like a foolish man who built his house on sand. The rain came down, the streams rose, and the winds blew and beat against that house, and it fell with a great crash"* (Matthew 7:24–27).
- *Read:* Isaiah 28:16–17

QUESTIONS TO PONDER

- Have you ever experienced a situation in which you realized your foundation wasn't as strong as you'd thought? What changes occurred in your life as a direct result?
- How did that experience change your understanding of the word *trust*?

WEEKLY CONNECTION IDEA

Put your faith into action. Volunteer as a group for an organization that helps to rebuild the lives and faith of individuals.

WEEK 4   DAY 1: REAL ME

After a trip to the grocery store, I was putting everything away and noticed that a hinge on our pantry door was squeaking. Every time I opened the door to put away something else, I heard this horrible, long screech. I couldn't find the WD-40®, so I hurriedly finished the put-away task, not wanting to hear the noise anymore.

Unfortunately, the hinge continued to make its annoying noise all that day. I didn't realize how much I opened and closed the pantry door until I had that ridiculous sound keeping count. It seemed like we'd just oiled the hinges of that door. But when

I thought about it, I realized it really had been a while. Time had just gotten away from me.

I actually notice something similar about myself too. If I don't pour in the oil of the Word on a consistent basis and stay tuned in to the sound of God's voice, I, myself, can become a little squeaky—hard to be around, annoying, bothersome. I start to act a lot less out of love and a lot more out of the dryness of my heart—that can be really noisy. Touching base with God every now and then is really not enough to keep things moving smoothly.

I found some oil and applied it to the hinges; now the door opens as smoothly as silk. I also started spending more time in the Word on a consistent basis, and I'm keeping it handy for whenever things start to get a little squeaky. Everyone around here has been glad on both counts.

After all, there's nothing like a little peace and quiet.

- *If I could speak all the languages of earth and of angels, but didn't love others, I would only be a noisy gong or a clanging cymbal* (1 Corinthians 13:1 NLT).
- *Read:* Psalm 19:14, 2 Timothy 1:13

QUESTIONS TO PONDER
- What are your personal signs that your heart is getting "dry"?
- How does your perspective change when you are consistently in God's Word?

WEEKLY CONNECTION IDEA
As a group, decide on a daily Bible reading plan for all to do. Schedule a daily or weekly check-in via text message, email, or phone call to tell what passage meant most to each of you and why.

WEEK 4   DAY 2: REAL GRACE

Melinda shared another story:

> I spied the little guy in the early morning light. Sitting there on the skimmer shelf of the pool, with its little nose struggling to stay above the water line, was a field

mouse. It looked exhausted, its coat matted together like it had been trying to get out of the water all night.

Living creatures tend to scurry around our pool area at night. No fence or other barrier is there to stop small animals before they get to the water. From their vantage point in the darkness, they probably don't see anything at all until they've fallen right in the pool. Typically, the pool turns out to be their last stop. While the discovery of floating wildlife was nothing new to me, the experience of finding a *live* mouse in the pool *was*.

Kevin walked out about that time, and upon seeing the mouse, grabbed the pool net and said, "Buddy, today's your lucky day."

He took the end of the net and nudged the mouse off the shelf, back into the water, where it swam like crazy. Then, with one quick scoop, Kevin pulled the mouse from the water and pitched it back, away (way away!) from the house. I saw where the mouse landed and watched it run like the wind into the woods.

The mouse's plight made me think of how often we lose focus and start walking in the darkness where we can't really see what traps and dangers lurk ahead. When we've suddenly fallen into a crazy pit, we don't cry out for help. We struggle and struggle to get out on our own. *We* could *die there without help getting out.*

It's the smart mouse that allows itself to be nudged off the shelf of perceived safety to attain certain rescue.

It's the smart person who lets go for the same reason.

Be thankful. Help is available. Today could be your lucky day.

- *He lifted me out of the slimy pit, out of the mud and mire; he set my feet on a rock and gave me a firm place to stand* (Psalm 40:2).
- *Read:* Pull me from the trap my enemies set for me, for I find protection in you alone
- Psalm Psalm 18:19, 31:4

QUESTIONS TO PONDER

- How tightly do you hold the control of your life? Do you often try to get yourself out of your own messes because you're either afraid to let go or feel you don't deserve God's help?

- Think of a time when you actually did let go and let God. Write what you learned from it and how it has affected your choices during subsequent times you've needed God's help and grace. If you have never let go, pray for God to show you how.

WEEK 4   DAY 3: REAL FELLOWSHIP

A chair sits in front of my desk, as is the case with many desks in many offices. This chair is a small wingback with slightly out-of-date upholstery, and it's not particularly comfortable. However, it is rarely empty.

That chair seems to make persons want to sit and linger. They start out waiting for their appointment, and once that's over, some come and sit for a while longer. They'll walk past the doorway and stop to sit for a few minutes to say hello. Nine times out of ten, they'll start talking about their families, their work and dreams, or their failures and triumphs.

There's just something about that chair.

We spend an awful lot of time closed off in our society today, whether it's behind a computer or invisible walls we've constructed to keep people out. Most of the time, we just like to keep our heads down and do what we have to do to get through a day. We don't like to get involved because it could come back to bite us, so we avoid eye contact altogether.

A little something dies inside us when we make this our common practice. Human interaction is to our souls like Miracle-Gro® is to our plants. We can get along without it, but we will be less developed a person, and our lives less vibrant. We start to wither sooner, instead of blooming to the very end of our season.

Perhaps we all need to go through each day acting as though we have an empty chair sitting across from us. Maybe we should make a practice of looking up and catching a person's eye, inviting them to sit for a while, and daring to get involved.

What's the worst that could happen?

Well, true, you might not get much work done, but you'd feel your heart expanding like a Grinch at Christmas. And who *knows* what would happen if you reupholstered?

- *Rejoice with those who rejoice, weep with those who weep* (Romans 12:15 ESV).
- *Read:* 1 Thessalonians 5:11, James 1:19

QUESTIONS TO PONDER
- Do you often miss opportunities to reach out to others because of distractions that keep your focus elsewhere? If you are honest, what is the key issue that keeps you from reaching out?
- Can you think of any individuals whom God has placed right in your path for interaction? Select at least one, and make contact this week.

WEEK 4   DAY 4: REAL FRIENDSHIP

I love my friends who are my own age, but I have a special appreciation for those who are older. We all need the perspective from persons who have "been there" and know the way to where we're going. With their input, we can travel a little easier because they can warn us about the potholes and the detours and help keep us on the right road. And as we turn the tables and share with those who are younger, we can rejoice in our triumphs and tell of our mistakes to help others avoid them altogether. It is wonderful when we can make our mistakes count for good.

Whether you enter into a formal mentoring relationship or just sit down to get your nails done, you have *a lot* to offer. Never buy into the lie that you don't. Whether you have good life stories or harrowing tales of woe, God uses them all to pull us beyond ourselves and straight into the hearts of others.

It's a blessing as rich as those two heavy accents discussing an almighty God.

- *You, however, must teach what is appropriate to sound doctrine. Teach the older men to be temperate, worthy of respect, self-controlled, and sound in faith, in love and in endurance.*

Likewise, teach the older women to be reverent in the way they live, not to be slanderers or addicted to much wine, but to teach what is good. Then they can urge the younger women to love their husbands and children, to be self-controlled and pure, to be busy at home, to be kind, and to be subject to their husbands, so that no one will malign the word of God.

Similarly, encourage the young men to be self-controlled. In everything set them an example by doing what is good. In your teaching show integrity, seriousness and soundness of speech that cannot be condemned, so that those who oppose you may be ashamed because they have nothing bad to say about us (Titus 2:1–8).

• *Read:* Romans 8:28

QUESTIONS TO PONDER

• Please revisit this. Who serves as a mentor to you? If you don't have a mentor yet, ask God to bring to mind some older women who might be willing to invest in you. Remember, older in their spiritual walk is just as beneficial as older in age.

• Authenticity is paramount in a mentoring friendship. How does sharing the less stellar parts of your life benefit both parties?

WEEKLY CONNECTION IDEA

Head out as a group to get your nails done. Brainstorm on ways to coordinate with your church or in your community to mentor younger women.

WEEK 4   DAY 5: REAL FAITH

I love cute little shops. My town has quite a few—some filled with antiques, others with gifts and home decor, and many with trendy women's clothing. Another thing you might notice in our area is what is commonly known as cowboy values. Cowboys are not just a hard-working bunch; they love their Jesus more than their favorite saddle or pair of Lucchese cowboy boots. The towns are laced with Cowboy churches and iron cutouts of cowboys kneeling before the Cross, their noble steeds at their sides. That love is reflected on everything from frames and hats, to artwork and dishware, and even to clothing.

A lot of it is really cute, but then there were the shorts I saw in a shop window. They were denim cutoffs, covered in black crosses of varying sizes appliquéd on the front and back, with the largest one displayed prominently on the left buttock and glitzed up with rhinestone beading so you couldn't miss it. As if you could have. Seeing these shorts and other decorative references to the Cross made me wonder if God really needs the PR that badly. Maybe He would rather we just put on Jesus Himself. Instead of covering our homes, accessories, and selves with the image of the cross, maybe He'd just rather us let Christ Himself shine through us, brighter than all that Texas glitz. Perhaps that would draw people to Him a lot faster than a cross sparkling on our behinds (Really, I think that just draws people to our behinds, alone, but that might just be me.)

Please know that I'm not against cute Christian-themed stuff. I own some of it, and I love to wear my various cross necklaces. I enjoy browsing through shops that sell that stuff. I think it pleases God to see us displaying our faith, but only as long as we remember to wear our Lord Jesus Christ most prominently of all. The light of Him should be drawing people straight to His heart. If it is, I'm thankful to say, nothing will be able to distract them from it. Well, maybe those shorts could.

Let's just all rethink stuff like those shorts.

- *Rather, clothe yourselves with the Lord Jesus Christ* (Romans 13:14).
- *Read:* Matthew 5:14–16, Colossians 3:10–11

QUESTIONS TO PONDER

- It is so easy to allow our outward appearance or our list of Christian accolades tell the tale of a "strong" faith. But real faith is evidenced from the heart. Can you identify someone you know whose authentic faith shines through without any additional "help"? Write about that person.
- What are the key factors that build an authentic faith?

Bible Study On the Go!

Interact. Engage. Grow.

New Hope Interactive is a new digital Bible study platform that allows you to unlock content to download your favorite New Hope Bible study workbooks on your tablet or mobile device. Your answers and notes are kept private through a profile that's easy to create and FREE!

Perfect for individual or small group use!

To learn more visit NewHopeInteractive.com/getstarted